Genealogist's
for
Upper Saint John Valley
Research

by
George L. Findlen

CLEARFIELD

Printed for
Clearfield Company, Inc. by
Genealogical Publishing Co., Inc.
Baltimore, Maryland
2003

International Standard Book Number: 0-8063-5207-8

Made in the United States of America

Table of Contents

Table of Contents
(Continued)

Upper Saint John River Valley
Communities
(west)

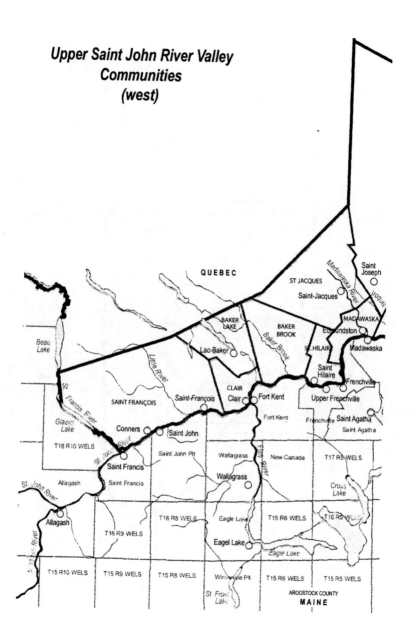

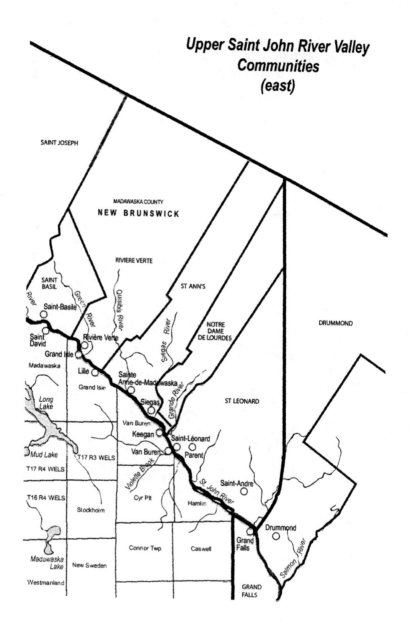

Upper Saint John River Valley Communities (east)

SAINT JOSEPH

MADAWASKA COUNTY
NEW BRUNSWICK

RIVIERE VERTE

SAINT BASIL

ST ANN'S

Saint-Basile

NOTRE DAME DE LOURDES

DRUMMOND

Saint David

Rivière Verte

Grand Isle

Madawaska

Lille

Sainte Anne-de-Madawaska

Grand Isle

Siegas

ST LEONARD

Long Lake

Van Buren

Keegan

Saint-Léonard

Mud Lake

T17 R3 WELS

Van Buren

Parent

T17 R4 WELS

Saint-Andre

T16 R4 WELS

Cyr Plt

Hamlin

Stockholm

Drummond

Connor Twp

Caswell

Grand Falls

Madawaska Lake

New Sweden

Westmanland

GRAND FALLS

Green River, *Quisibis River*, *Siegas River*, *Grande River*, *Violette Brook*, *St. John River*, *Salmon River*

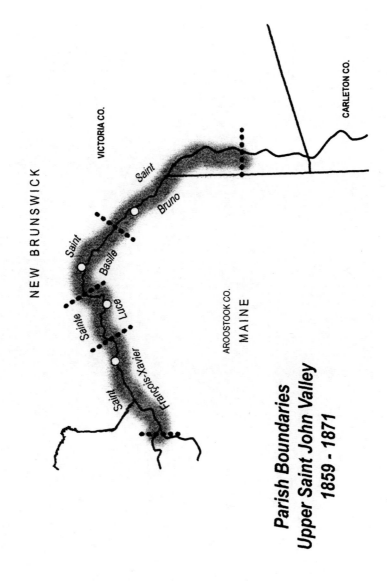

NEW BRUNSWICK

VICTORIA CO.

CARLETON CO.

AROOSTOOK CO.

MAINE

Saint

Saint

Bruno

Basile

Saint

Luce

Sainte

François-Xavier

Saint

Parish Boundaries
Upper Saint John Valley
1859 - 1871

Acknowledgments

No work of this nature is possible without the considerable help of archive and library staff and of state agency and provincial office employees who serve the public. It is thanks to all of them that this work exists.

A special thanks is due to Nicholas Hawes, assistant director of the Acadian Archives at the University of Maine at Fort Kent. He read the entire manuscript of an early draft and made detailed suggestions for improving every section of this book. The book is considerably better because of his efforts.

Other individuals who have made a contribution to this book are thanked in the section they helped me with.

Introduction

Economic necessity has dispersed many descendants of the original families who settled in the Upper Saint John Valley. Some of those families had been there since the mid-1780s. Again and again those who do genealogy on Valley families hear, "How can I find information on my family's ancestors?" This monograph is an attempt to answer that question for the many, both from near by and from far away, who wish to identify their Valley ancestors and find out as much as they can about them.

Current handbooks in the field of genealogy focus on large geographic areas, usually no smaller than a single state or province. As a result, the resources of a smaller geographic area are frequently ignored. In the case of the Upper Saint John River Valley, the resources are rich enough and the interest by descendants is ample enough to warrant the separate attention of this monograph. In addition, by focusing on a smaller geographic area, more attention can be given to detail than in books on larger geographic areas.

The focus of this guide is on the individuals who settled in the Madawaska Settlement beginning with the blended Acadian / French-Canadian families who moved there in 1785. Initially, "the Madawaska Settlement" meant the land along both sides of the Saint John River between the Madawaska River and the Green River (Rivière Verte). Soon, it included everything on both sides of the Saint John River "between the two falls," that is, from Edmundston (the Little Falls) to Grand Falls. In time, it stretched from Grand Falls to the Allagash. In order to make this work manageable, its focus will be on resources for finding families who lived between the community of Drummond immediately southeast of Grand Falls at the east end to Allagash Township just beyond the mouth of the Saint Francis River at the west end. It will also include the Fish River and its supplying lakes in the south-central part of the Valley and the Madawaska River up to Lake Témouiscata at the northwest end. The resources in this guide and the families they cover are within an arc some 80 miles long and about 20 miles wide.

On the American side, townships dealt with in this monograph include those of Allagash, Caswell, Cyr, Eagle Lake, Fort Kent, Frenchville, Grand Isle, Hamlin, Madawaska, New Canada, Saint John, Saint Francis, Sainte Agathe, Sinclair, Van Buren, and Wallagrass. On the Canadian side, communities dealt with in this monograph include those of Baker Brook, Clair, Connors, Drummond, Edmundston, Grand Falls, Lac Baker, Notre Dame de Lourdes (Siegas), Rivière Verte, Saint André, Saint Basile, Saint François, Saint Hilaire, Saint Jacques, Saint Joseph, Saint Léonard, and Sainte Anne.

The Valley has been home to Malecites, Acadians, French-Canadians, Yankees, Irish, a few Scots, and a few Loyalists (mostly English). By virtue of the fact that the blended Acadian / French-Canadian families are most numerous, it will appear that they get the most attention. However, searchers will find their non-French ancestors in Valley resources. For Catholic families (primarily Maliseets, Acadians, French-Canadians, and most Irish), church registers are the richest source of information, and this guide gives them much attention. Non-Catholic families (primarily Yankees, Loyalists, Scots, and some Irish), with the exception of Anglican and Presbyterian families in the Edmundston area, must focus on land records (after 1845 on the southern side, after 1848 on the northern side), publically collected vital records (starting in 1892 on the southern side, starting in 1886 on the northern side), and census records (especially after 1850 on the south side and after 1851 on the north side) to document their families. These land records, vital records, and census returns are described in this guide.

This guide includes both those resources that can be found only in the Valley itself and those resources found at major archives outside the Valley. The emphasis, however, is on resources available in the Valley, a few of which can be found only there. Resources are equally rich on both sides of the Valley. Thus, this monograph gives as much attention to resources found in Aroostook County, Maine, as it does to resources found in Madawaska County and the western edge of Victoria County, New Brunswick. Since families who trace themselves to the Valley had ancestors who lived on both sides of the river, searchers should become familiar with and use resources on both sides of the river.

Excluding histories and published lists of marriages, the time period covered by the documentary resources described in this guide goes from 1792, when the church of Saint Basile began its register, until well into the 20th century. The dates covered by a given resource depend on what that resource is and on government laws governing the availability of public documents.

Two groups of readers are envisioned for this guide. The first group is made up of residents of the Valley who may not be fully aware of all the resources available there. For them, this guide is a full listing of those resources and an encouragement to use all of them. Those who bother to go beyond a listing of names and dates will uncover a rich store of information about their ancestors' lives. The second group of readers envisioned for this guide is made up of descendants who live far away and would like information on how to locate information about their ancestors that is available to them at home and during visits to the Valley. It is with them in mind that location descriptions are provided.

Historical Overview

Prior to the summer of 1785, when the first 16 or so blended Acadian and French-Canadian families arrived to stay, the Upper Saint John River Valley was part of the hunting ground of the Maliseet Indians. Given the geography of the Maritimes, the Saint John and Madawaska Rivers were nature's highway between Halifax and Québec and later between Saint John and Québec. Acadian messengers ("couriers"—literally "runners") made the trip regularly.

It would appear that some Acadian families dispersed from Nova Scotia by the Deportation settled in the Lower Valley near Saint Ann's Point (today's Fredericton, NB), in or before 1755. Burned out by Mozes Hazzen's rangers in 1758, these families escaped to the Québec area via the Saint John and Madawaska Rivers by using the known Indian portage overland from Lake Témouiscata to Rivière-du-Loup on the Saint Lawrence, thence up to Québec. There, a number of them married French-Canadians on Île d'Orléans, at Sainte-Anne-de-la-Pocatière, and at Kamouraska. In 1768, some of these families returned to French Village, about 7 miles upstream from Saint Anne's Point, and other Acadian and French-Canadian families joined them. They likely traveled back by the same route they had used when fleeing ten years earlier. The American colonies revolted eight years later in 1776, and several of these individuals served as messengers and scouts for the British.

After the American War of Independence ended in 1783, the King of England had the problem of what to do with American colonists who had fought for the Crown. The solution was to remove and resettle them. A large number of them were resettled on the lower Saint John River. Some 1,300 New Jersey Volunteers, men, women, and children, were granted lands in the French Village area. The large influx of Loyalists from the former colonies—14,000 in all—pushed the British government to make New Brunswick a separate province a year later. The resettled Loyalists got government land grants; French "squatters" were permitted to sell their "improvements." A few years earlier, government messenger Louis Mercure had tried to sell the governors of Upper Canada and of Lower Canada on the idea of giving grants of land to those wanting to settle in the Madawaska area as a way of helping to keep the only land route open for communication. The alternative communication link was a long sail around Nova Scotia, Cape Breton Island, Prince Edward Island, and the long Gaspé peninsula. When tensions developed between the French, who had been there for 15 years, and the newly arrived Loyalists, who needed to make a start, the governor of the newly created province of New Brunswick adopted Mercure's idea and 24 families were told that they would be given grants if they developed lots. His motive appears to be to affirm that the Madawaska region was part of the new province, not part of Québec, and to keep the communication line with Québec open by stationing people along the route.

Most—not all—French left the area, some for Miramichi Bay and other places along New Brunswick's eastern coastline, others for the Madawaska area farther up the Saint John River. To get a grant, they had to clear and work at least three acres, and they had to maintain three cattle per every 50 acres. In lieu of cultivating the land, they could mine it. If they did not work the land, they had to build a 20' x 16' dwelling and maintain three cattle per each 50 acres. The land clearing or building had to be done within three years of receiving the grant.

In the summer of 1785, an estimated 16 families paddled up the river, portaged around the big falls, and pulled off at a location below the little falls, roughly behind today's church of Saint David just east of the current town of Madawaska. A granite cross now marks the general location that oral history, passed down by the descendants of the first families, claims they landed. Families took up lots on either side of the river and began to clear land. Other families followed in the next 20 years. In addition, other families with kinship ties to these families moved to the Valley from the lower Saint Lawrence, forming about a third of the population by 1800. Almost all new families to the Valley thereafter were from Québec, from the Kennebec River Valley, or were immigrant Irish who arrived in New Brunswick between 1820 and 1850.

In 1790, the New Brunswick government issued grants for lots of land on both sides of the Saint John River between the Little Falls on the Madawaska River down to the mouth of the Green River. Lots followed the French model. They were narrow, had river frontage, and went one-mile in depth. A cart path developed parallel to the river connecting farm to farm. Until the railroad came in the 1870s on the Canadian side and in the 1890s on the American side, the Madawaska and Saint John Rivers and secondary roads were the primary means for the transportation of goods to and from the settlement.

As the transcript of an 1828 trial shows, these families always believed they were British citizens. They voted, paid taxes, used the New Brunswick court system, and served in the provincial militia. The American government seemed not to be aware of them until that year.

The Valley has been home to Acadians, French-Canadians, Yankees, Irish, and English. The Acadians were from what is today known as Nova Scotia, and the first group to settle in the Valley had come from French Village just above today's Fredericton. Most had married French-Canadians during the deportation years from the Bas Saint Laurent.

In 1818, that changed when several Kennebec County families came north looking for virgin pine to cut. The Americans, led by agitator John Baker, maintained that all land south of the Notre Dame Mountains on the southern edge of the Saint Lawrence was American in accordance with the 1783 treaty which ended what the Americans called the War of Independence and what the British called the American War of Rebellion. New Brunswick officials claimed that the entire Valley always had been and continued to be British. Baker's actions led to his arrest for "high misdemeanors" in 1827. The State of Maine, separated from Massachusetts as part of the Missouri Compromise of 1820, was livid.

Both national governments tried to maintain good relations through the period, and efforts to settle the border issue, which both sides worked at off and on since 1783, continued without success. A flare-up occurred ten years later in 1838 as more and more settlers came to the area and as two growing populations tried to claim and harvest the large supply of virgin pine. Each side attempted to stop the other from moving timber, and a number of arrests were made. This time, Maine was ready to go to war, and it took the efforts of General Winfield Scott, sent by the US president Martin Van Buren, to calm things down. The forts at Fort Fairfield and Fort Kent on the American side and at Edmundston and Cabano on the Canadian side date from this period of the Bloodless Aroostook War. Maine separated its vast northern wilderness into a separate Aroostook County, which still occupies 25% of the land mass of the state. It is also at this time that Maine authorized the building of a road from the mouth of the Mattawamkeg River on the Penobscott through the wilderness to the small community of Houlton, which had been settled by American Revolutionary War soldiers given grants of land in lieu of pay. No road farther north would be authorized until after the border was settled in 1842.

Since its humble beginnings in 1785, the Acadian and French-Canadian population had grown, and young men cleared "second range" lots behind their fathers' original river lots. Others spread up or down the Saint John River, buying improvements from men who had started clearing or making stakes of their own. In October 1825, Maine and Massachusetts had given deeds to John Baker and neighbor John Bacon as a way of asserting their claim on the land, causing a minor international furor. In the interests of peace, both national governments agreed to stop issuing grants until the boundary was settled. Time did not stand still for the diplomats, however. Children continued to be born, and young men grew up and needed to support new families. So Valley families acted without deeds in the interim.

In 1842, the American and British governments finally agreed on an international boundary in spite of Maine's vigorous and vociferous disagreement with it. The border went right through the center of the Saint John River as far west as the Saint Francis River. All Acadian and French-Canadian families living south of the River since 1785 became American; their brothers and sisters on living north of the River remained Canadian. Settlers were rightfully worried about the title to their farms. However, by treaty terms, designed to "quiet settlers' claims," all who had received a grant by either government would have their grant validated by the government now holding the land, and all who had a possessory claim received a grant. Both governments sent teams to survey land claims. On the American side, a survey was done in 1843 and deeds were issued in 1845. Deeds were issued in 1848 on the Canadian side.

The culture of Valley families, however, remained intact. People continued to cross the river to work, date, and marry, and Catholic churches on both sides of the river remained part of a Canadian diocese. Only in 1870 would Pope Pius IX make all American-side parishes part of the Diocese of Portland. In time, the automobile and railroad, the universal military draft, and the radio resulted in an amalgamation of Valley residents with people outside the Valley. In spite of this cultural mingling, almost all Valley families have one or more descendent lines still residing in the Valley, making it possible for searchers to trace their family's history for at least 200 years using only those genealogical resources found within the Valley itself.

By the third quarter of the 19th century, loggers found the supply of virgin timber was not infinite, and larger operations moved west into New York, Michigan, Wisconsin, and Minnesota where descendants of some Valley families can be found to this day. Soil that was so rich for farming immediately after the virgin pine was removed eventually eroded, parts of the Valley having poor, gravelly soil. A post-World War II national economy that encouraged farmers to abandon self-sustaining farming in the late 1940s for a single cash crop of potatoes and a 21st-century international economy suffering from overproduction due to technological developments have forced most Upper Saint John Valley farmers out of farming. The population peaked in the 1950s, but an out-migration of residents, started two decades earlier during the Great Depression, has continued unabated. In the year 2000, there were fewer residents in Aroostook County, Maine, and in Madawaska County, New Brunswick, than there were 50 years earlier.

Histories

To locate and trace the movement of our Acadian and French-Canadian ancestors, one must understand what has happened to the people who settled in the Valley. For that, one must read their story. A number of books can help. They will come in handy when searchers try to tell their own family's story.

The books listed below are organized into three groupings. The first grouping deals with the people who settled in the Upper Saint John Valley: the Maliseets, Acadians, French-Canadians, Yankees, and Irish. A family's story is intimately entwined with the story of the group that settled in the Valley. The second grouping deals with political geography: Québec, New Brunswick, and Maine. As isolated as the Upper Saint John Valley was, government and commerce kept it connected to the world around it, and the events which shaped these two provinces and one state have made their contributions to the story of every family in the Valley. The third grouping deals with the Valley's story itself and with the stories of its individual church parishes and towns. These parishes and towns are the smallest social units in which a family's story has evolved. Family historians should understand how each has effected a given family's own history.

For those who live many provinces and states away from the Valley, the books listed below may be found through rare book dealers, in major genealogical research centers in the United States and Canada, at several locations in the Upper Saint John Valley described below in the Archives and in the Libraries sections, and at rare book dealers (such as www.bookfinder.com and www.abebooks.com, which are only two of the many available). Searchers who live near the Valley should check several electronic library catalogues to locate a copy at one of the libraries in the Valley. URSUS (http://130.111.64.31) is the electronic catalog shared by University of Maine System campuses (including the Acadian Archives), the Maine State Archives, the Maine State Library, and the Bangor Public Library. The holdings of public libraries on the Canadian side can be searched at vision.gnb.ca. Finally, the Centre de Documentation et d'Études Madawaskayenne holdings can be searched via its web site at www.cuslm.ca/cedem. (At the site, click on "Livres et périodiques" then on a subject heading. Once at a list, either scroll down the long page or use the web browser's Edit and Find-and-Replace features to locate a given author or title.) Readers living far away from the Valley should note that the archives described below do not participate in the interlibrary loan program, but other libraries in the US and Canada having these titles do.

The titles that follow may not be the best options available. They are provided as introductions. Curious readers will want to turn to the bibliographies in these books to find more titles.

The People

Maliseets

Prior to the arrival of any Europeans, the Maliseets lived in the entire Saint John River Valley and all its tributary river valleys. Their homelands extended from the mouth of the Saint John River, through the Madawaska River to Lake Témiscouata, and on to Rivière du Loup on the Saint Lawrence. They also hunted and fished the Fish River and its many feeder lakes, the Aroostook River Valley, the Tobique River, and the Kennebecasis River. The following will introduce searchers to these original inhabitants of the Upper Saint John Valley.

> Erickson, Vincint O. "Maliseet-Passamaquoddy." In *Handbook of North American Indians*, edited by William C. Sturtevant. Vol. 15. Washington, D.C.: Smithsonian, 1978.

This reputable encyclopedia entry has sections on language, territory, history, culture, and recent developments. Nearly a full page is devoted to a description of additional information.

Acadians

The first European-origin families to move to and remain in the Upper Saint John Valley were Acadians who had intermarried with French-Canadians during the deportation years. The following two works provide family historians with an introduction to the Acadian portion of their family's history.

> Arsenault, Bona. *History of the Acadians*. Saint-Laurent, Quebec: Fides, 1994.

This is a translation of volume 1 of Arsenault's earlier multi-volume work, published in 1955 under the title, *L'Acadie des Ancêtres*, and revised for his very successful two-volume, *Histoire et Généalogie des Acadiens* (1965). Although not a professional historian, he is quite accurate in his details. Genealogists will like the work since he sprinkles family names throughout. He starts with the founding of Port Royal in Acadie (Port Annapolis, Nova Scotia) and ends with their resettlement efforts following the deportation of 1755 and the conquest of Canada by the British in 1763. The book has a good index. It ends with a five page bibliography and a two-page list of key words that English-speaking genealogists should have at their elbow whenever reading a church register or other historical document written in French. The book is available in libraries and from rare book dealers. The English translation(history only)and the two-volume French version(history with genealogy) are both available at the University of Maine at Presque Isle and at the Acadian Archives at the University of Maine at Fort Kent.

> Ross, Sally, and Alphonse Deveau. *The Acadians of Nova Scotia, Past and Present*. Halifax, Nova Scotia: Nimbus, 1992.

This award-winning short history is both well-researched and readable. Acadian descendants wanting to get a start on their history would do well to begin with Ross and Deveau. The book has two halves, the history of Acadia up to the deportation (past), and a short history of each post-deportation Acadian community in Nova Scotia (present).

Readers will find the first half, only 70 pages long, an easy read. Notes at the end of the three history chapters lead readers to more books as does the bibliography at the end. It is available at the Acadian Archives at the University of Maine at Fort Kent.

French Canadians

After the initial blended Acadian/French-Canadian families moved to the Upper Saint John valley from French Village near today's Fredericton, French-Canadian families, many of whom were related by marriage to Acadian families in the valley, themselves moved to the valley. By 1800, 20% of the families in the Valley had come from the Bas Saint Laurent area, today's Kamouraska, Témiscouata, Rivière du Loup, and l'Islet Counties. The following book will give searchers an introduction to the French-Canadian portion of their family's history.

Frenette, Yves. *Brève Histoire des Canadiens Français*. Montréal: Boréal, 1998.

This 197-page book, written in French, has chapters on the birth of a people, 1535-1760; under the shadow of conquerers, 1760-1840; the unification of French Canada, 1840-1918; roads of difference, 1918-1967; and identities and conflict, 1967-present. It is easy to read and historically sound.

Yankees

With the arrival of the Baker family in 1818, Americans from the Kennebeck River Valley became residents of the Upper Saint John River Valley. Some of those families remained after the prime lumber was gone and after the boundary dispute was settled. The following book will introduce searchers to the region they came from.

Calvert, Mary R. *The Kennebeck Wilderness Awakens*. Lewiston, Maine: Twin City Printery, 1986.

This is the follow up of Calvert's earlier 1983 title, Dawn Over the Kennebec. Although this is not a book about the people as a group, it includes references to the major figures in the history of the Valley's development. A whole chapter is devoted to lumbering, and several places deal with the French Canadians who eventually became the majority residents of Lewiston and Waterville.

Irish

The Irish immigration to North America took place all through the 19th century. The Port of Saint John, NB, was a regular destination for immigrant ships seeking lumber for the return cargo. Many Irish landing at Saint John went up river to the Aroostook and to the Grand Falls area. The following will introduce searchers to the Irish who came to New Brunswick.

Hynes, Leo J. *The Catholic Irish in New Brunswick: a History of Their Prominent Role in the Shaping of the Province and the Structuring of the Roman Catholic Church*. Moncton, New Brunswick: L. J. Hynes, 1992.

This popular history is divided into parts on Saint John and Southern New Brunswick, Fredericton and the Saint John River, and Miramichi North and East New Brunswick. The author devotes a whole chapter on Grand Falls. Its strength is that it

7

contains a lot of names of individuals and describes the contribution of each to the history of the Province. Unfortunately, it has no index. Three pages of bibliography lead readers to other books dealing with the Irish in New Brunswick.

The Political Geography

Family history does not exist in a vacuum. Families live in counties that are part of a state or province that is part of a country. What has happened in the larger contexts of Québec, New Brunswick, and Maine has impacted individual families living in the villages and on the farms of the Upper Saint John Valley. The following three works will introduce genealogists to those larger contexts.

Québec

During the Grand Dérangement years, many Acadian families managed to get to Québec area. There, they intermarried with French Canadians. After they relocated in the French Village area near today's Fredericton, they remained in touch. After some of them relocated to the Madawaska Settlement, relatives from the lower Saint Lawrence also moved to the Settlement. The following is a short history of all of Québec.

Hamlin, Jean, and Jean Provencher. *Brève Histoire de Québec*. Rev. ed. Montréal: Boréal, 1997.

This 130-page popular work has been around for ten years and still sells well. Written in French by respected historians, it is divided into three parts: New France, 1608-1763; One Régime to Another, 1763-1868; and Modern Québec, 1868-1985.

New Brunswick

Within two years of the Loyalists' arrival, the large number of them justified their separation into a separate provice. Thus, New Brunswick was born in the same year that the original Acadian and French-Canadian families moved from the Fredericton area to the Madawaska Settlement. The following is a short history of the province.

Frink, Tim. *New Brunswick: a Short History*. Saint John, New Brunswick: Stonington Books, 1997.

This 152-page work has chapters on First Settlers, Boundaries, the Acadian Expulsions, the English, the Loyalists, and the Irish. Unfortunately, it has no index.

Maine

The newest of the political entities directly effecting valley families, Maine was separated from Massachusetts as part of the Missouri Compromise of 1820. The following is Maine's story.

Rolde, Neil. *Maine: A Narrative History*. Gardiner, Maine: Harpswell Press, 1990.

Most of Maine's history deals with its older and more populated southern part of the state, and this work reflects those two facts.

The Valley

Family history is inherently local, and those who construct the story of their ancestral families must become familiar with the history of the specific locales in which they lived. The following works will introduce individuals to events within the Valley proper, the scene of their family's story.

> Mercure, Prudent. *Papiers de/Papers of Prudent L. Mercure; Histoire du Madawaska.* Edited by Roger Paradis. Madawaska, Maine: Madawaska Historical Society, 1998.

Serious students and researchers of Acadians and French-Canadians in the Upper Saint John Valley will find this work indispensable. It contains all of the many documents that Prudent Mercure collected plus a few that Roger Paradis has added. Paradis has spent years editing Mercure's three volumes and the effort shows . His 70-page introductory history is excellent, replacing much of what Fr. Albert did, and his 50-page bibliography is quite inclusive. The book is available at the University of Maine campuses at Fort Kent and Presque Isle, and at the University of Moncton at Edmundston. It is available for sale from the Madawaska Historical Society.

> Albert, Thomas. *The History of Madawaska: An English Translation.* Translated by Francis Doucette and Therese Doucette. Madawaska, Maine: Madawaska Historical Society, 1989.

This is the second edition of a translation by a brother-and-sister team of Father Albert's book, originally published in French in 1920. The book's origin is almost as fascinating reading as the material within it. It is based on the collection efforts of Prudent Mercure who once wanted to write the history of the Madawaska Settlement and, while working as a Canadian government archivist, made copies of many documents pertaining to the Upper Saint John Valley. Ill health forced him to sell his notebooks to an American who was one of the first Acadians from the Saint John Valley to sit in the Maine legislature. This legislator in turn begged Fr. Albert to write that history. Fr. Albert hesitantly agreed and made use of Mercure's notebooks as he wrote. The history has background information on the Valley's pre-European history and the reasons for the migration to Madawaska. It is the only attempt at a full history of the Madawaska area. Readers must be aware that, since Fr. Albert was not a professional historian, he is clearly biased in his views of those forces that have molded the history of the Valley. Chapter XI on Valley Catholic parishes is invaluable for the genealogist. (Readers will be confused when they read "IX" at the top of that page in the English translation.) For those who know where their ancestors lived, knowing when each church opened tells searchers when to stop looking for descendants in the register of one parish and when to begin looking in the register of another. Likewise, the author's Notes for Chapter IX reproduces the census made by Deane and Kavanagh in 1831. That report lists each resident, in order, from the Saint Francis River in the west to the international boundary line not far from Grand Falls in the east. Both the updated French version and the English translations are widely available. Copies are available on both sides of the river at almost every public library between Grand Falls and Fort Kent. The book is also available for purchase from the Madawaska Historical Society.

Melvin, Charlotte Lenentine. *Madawaska, A Chapter in Maine–New Brunswick Relations*. Madawaska, Maine: Madawaska Historical Society, 1975.

A thesis completed at the University of Rochester in 1956, Melvin's work has had a second life as a publication of the Madawaska Historical Society. She is a trained historian and has a gift for telling the story with a minimum of quotes from the original sources she uses. One of her appendices lists Duperre's list of 24 settlers who requested permission to move from Sainte-Anne-des-Pays-Bas (French Village, known as Kingsclear today) above Fredericton to the Madawaska area in 1785; another lists Odell's list of Original Settlers receiving a License of Occupation in 1787. Her chapter on Ecclesiastical Separation contains information that few pay attention to but that is useful to all genealogists. Although much of her work deals with the big picture of the frontier (which was not determined for the 59 years between the end of the War of Independence in 1783 and the Webster-Ashburton Treaty of 1842) and of the relationship between Maine and New Brunswick, she still gives a lot of space to the mostly Acadian population caught in between. The book is in the Special Collections of the University of Maine at Presque Isle Library and at the Centre de Documentation et d'Études Madawaskayenne. It is also for sale from the Madawaska Historical Society.

Dubay, Guy F. *Light on the Past: Documentation on Our Acadian Heritage*. Madawaska, Maine: 1994-1995 Madawaska Board of Selectmen, 1995.

This 71-page collection of maps, facts, and lists is taken from documents pertaining to the history of the Madawaska Settlement and is an abstract of a larger work which was part of an application for an Acadian National Park. Genealogists will find many relatives placed within time and place. The work can be found at the Acadian Archives and at the Centre de Documentation et d'Études Madawaskayenne.

Doty, C. Stewart. *Acadian Hard Times, The Farm Security Administration in Maine's St. John Valley, 1940-1943*. Photographs by John Collier, Jr., Jack Dalano, and Jack Walas. Orono, Maine: University of Maine Press, 1991.

This collection of photographs was made at the end of the Great Depression. However, the war-time production that benefitted the local economy of other towns and states did not reach this far north. Thus, the difficulties of families starting out in one of the concessions during the 1940s are captured with stark clarity in these photos. They are valuable for providing us with clues as to how some of our ancestors lived in the late 1800s and early 1900s. Individuals putting together family histories of the Brown, Daigle, Dufour, Dumond, Gagnon, Gendreau, Labbé, and Lévesque clans will find photos of relatives here. The editor's 43-page essay on the Valley Acadians during the 1930s is well worth the time to read for its insights into the people at that time. For those who have not lived through it, Doty chronicles and documents the effects of the boom or bust potato economy which began with the bust of the 1930's and continued thereafter, leading to the outward migration to industrial cities in lower New England states in the 1940s which continues to this day. The book is available at Acadian Archives, and from the University of Maine Press, 126A College Avenue, Orono ME 04473, 207-866-0573, www.umaine.edu/umpress.

Parish and Community Histories

Each town and parish, on both sides of the River, has published bi-centennial and/or centennial histories. Although uneven in quality, they almost always contain a thumbnail history of the locality as understood by residents at the time the booklet was put together. They are frequently useful for lists of priests, initial families, and photos of landmarks and families gathered up by loving volunteers. When readers come across them, they should evaluate them and make careful note of title and location for future reference. They are found at the public libraries on both sides of the river as well as at the Acadian Archives and the Centre de Documentation et d'Études Madawaskayenne. What follows is a partial list of those works organized by township or cummunity. Thanks go to Geraldine Chassé for sharing her private collection of these histories with me.

Pozzuto, Cecile Dufour, comp. *Madoueska'k, 1785 - 1985: A Pictorial History Recapturing the Past.* N.p., 1985.

American Side

Allagash

Kelley, Edith. *Bits and Pieces of Allagash History.* Madawaska, Maine: Allagash Historical Society, 1976.

Cyr Plantation

Levasseur, Alphy, comp. *Cyr Plantation Centennial, 1870-1970.* N.p., 1970.

Frenchville

Raymond, David R. *A History of Sainte Luce Parish, Upper Frenchville— Frenchville, Maine, 1843-1993.* N.p., 1985.

Underhill, Hal & Emma Martin, comp. *A History of Frenchville.* N.p.: Frenchville Historical Society, 1994.

Fort Kent

Centennial Booklet Committee. *Fort Kent Centennial, 1869-1969.* N.p., 1969.

Grand Isle

Carrier-Daigle, Jeannine, Laruette Carrier-Lavertu, and Guy F. Dubay. *Souvenir Album Homecoming '94, Grand Isle, Lille, et les Concessions.* Madawaska, Maine: Saint John Valley Publishing Company, 1994.

Madawaska

Comité du Livre-Souvenir. *Live Souvenir, Centenaire du Madawaska, 1873-1973.* N.p., 1973.

Sainte Agathe

Raymond, David R. *The History of Saint Agathe Parish.* N.p.: Saint Agatha Historical Society, 1999.

Saint David

Saint David Parish Centennial Committee. *Saint David Parish Centennial, 1871-1971.* Madawaska, Maine: *Saint John Valley Times,* 1971.

Van Buren

Pelletier, Martin, and Monica Dionne Ferretti. *Van Buren History*.
Madawaska, Maine: Saint John Valley Publishing Co., 1979.

Canadian Side

Drummond

Violette, Simon, comp. *Saint-Michel de Drummond: Cent Ans ça se Fête*.
N.p.: Comité de Centenaire, 1990.

Edmundston

Michaud, Guy R. *La Paroisse de l'Immaculée Conception, Edmundston, N.B.,
1880-1980*. N.p.: Guy R. Michaud, 1980.

Grand Falls/Grand-Sault

Marceau, Margaret, in collaboration with Patrick McCooey. *Grand Falls
Yesterdays: A History of Grand Falls*. 2nd ed. Grand Falls, New Brunswick:
Grand Falls Historical Society, 2001.

Assomption, 1868-1993. N.p., 1993.

Rivière Verte

Comité du Livre. *Histoire de Rivière-Verte*. N.p., 1978.

Saint André

Saint-André-de-Madawaska, 1904-1954. N.p., 1954.

Sainte Anne

Comité du Livre du Centenaire. *100 ans Sainte-Anne de Madawaska, 1872-
1972*. N.p., 1972.

Saint Basile

Desjardins, Georgette, ed. *Saint-Basile: Berceau du Madawasks, 1792-1992*.
Montréal: Méridien, 1992.

Saint-François

Albert, Jacques G. *Saint-François-de-Madawaska, 1859-1984*. Edmundston,
New Brunswick: le Madawaska, 1984.

Saint Jacques

Michaud, Guy R. *La Paroisse de Saint-Jacques, Nouveau-Brunswick*.
Edmundston, New Brunswick: 0+ditions Guy R. Michaud, 1988.

Saint Léonard

Cyr, Marguerite, ed. *Saint-Léonard-Parent: 130 ans d'histoire*. N.p., 1984.

Siegas

140 Ans d'Histoire Siegas, 1844 à 1984. N.p., 1984.

In addition to these printed histories, the Diocese of Edmundston web site, at www.diocese-edmundston.ca/annuaire/zones-pastorales-et-paroisses/ zones.pastorales.et.paroisses.htm, has a link to each of its pastoral deaneries, where visitors can click on the name of a parish and look at what parishioners have identified as key events in the parish's history.

Church Registers

Genealogy is first and foremost discovering and documenting three events (birth, marriage, and death) with two circumstances (place and date) for each individual who is a relative by blood or marriage. Ancestors of Acadians, French-Canadians, and many of the Irish who moved to the Upper Saint John Valley were Roman Catholic, and church registers have been maintained for them with few major interruptions since 1702 (since 1620 for some Canadian families). They are, without doubt, the best source of information about baptism (birth), marriage, and burial (death) for those seeking information about their ancestors in the Upper Saint John Valley. Any person wanting information about a family with roots in the Valley should start with church registers.

In the case of Protestants who moved into the Valley, except for parishioners of Saint John the Baptist Anglican and Saint Paul's UCC, both in Edmundston, searchers will need to depend on census returns or vital records.

Church registers are invaluable precisely because they almost always contain the information genealogists need about family connections: identifying who the parents are of a given person and who is married to whom. Furthermore, for baptisms and burials, church registers almost always provide the date of birth or death. Finally, we can glean suggestions of family and neighborhood ties by noting the names of godparents for baptisms, witnesses for weddings, witnesses for burials, and from where an individual comes.

An important caveat must be mentioned regarding the identity of parents in marriage entries in Upper Saint John Valley parish registers. On the Canadian side, parents' names were usually not included in the entry between 1872 and 1893. On the American side, wherever Fr. Sweron served, between 1859 and 1900, parents' names were not included. Searchers will have to use census data or vital statistics required by the government (since 1886 in New Brunswick, since 1892 in Maine) to help make a case for a set of parents during these years.

Parish boundaries changed as the population grew. Understanding what was included in those boundaries and when they changed is important if genealogists are to know which parish register to examine. Genealogists should study closely the information below which lists when a parish began. Two examples should make the need to do this clear.

The first example involves the Bellefleur, Poitras, and Martin families who lived at the eastern end of the Valley in the civil parish of Saint Léonard. To find and document these families, searchers must start by looking in the register of Saint Basile, which was responsible for all the Valley until 1838. Then, searchers must shift to the register of Saint Bruno. Saint Bruno was responsible for both sides of the River from the Quisibis River about five miles (11 kilometers) west of today's Van Buren to at least as far east and south as Woodstock (later only to Tobique). For events starting in 1854, the searcher must shift again to the register of Saint Léonard-Parent, available on microfilm. In 1868, Saint

Léonard was separated from Saint Bruno and took over responsibility for the north side of the River from the Quisibis River down to within a mile of Grand Falls. In sum, one must look in three places for information on families who stayed in the same place.

The same is true at the western end of the Upper Saint John Valley, and my second example involves the Albert, Gagnon, and Ouellette families who lived near the current church of Saint Hilaire. Searchers must start with Saint Basile's registers from 1792 through 1842. Then they must turn to Sainte Luce in Frenchville. In 1868, in anticipation of Aroostook County(s becoming part of the Diocese of Portland, Maine, Saint Hilaire was separated from Sainte Luce, and searchers can again look up baptisms (births), marriage, and burials (deaths) on microfilm. Again, one must look in three places for information on families that did not move. Searchers who do not keep in mind the dates when a parish was founded will search in vain in the wrong location.

History of Catholic Parish Boundaries Upper Saint John Valley

Pre-Ecclesial Separation: 1792 - 1868/1871

Prior to roads, rivers were the means for moving from one place to another. Just as houses are built on both sides of a road today, houses were built on both sides of a river then. From its beginnings, the Madawaska Settlement included both sides of the Saint John River. Even the Webster-Ashburton Treaty of 1842 (known by the British as "The Treaty of Washington" since it was negotiated in Washington, D.C.), which set the international boundary in the center of the Saint John River, did not change how the people viewed themselves. Prior to 1868, each of the parishes listed below served families on both sides of the Saint John River.

Valley Center (Madawaska River to Quisibis River)

1792 - 1838.   Situated on the north shore of the Saint John River a few miles east of today's Edmundston, **Saint Basile** de Madawaska is the mother church for all Acadians, French Canadians, and Catholic Irish moving to the Upper Saint John Valley. Initially, the parish was responsible for serving the religious needs of individuals living anywhere in the Saint John River Valley, from the height of land above the south shore of the Saint Lawrence River northwest of Lake Témiscouata all the way down to Fredericton. It is the only church whose registers one needs to look in for documenting one's ancestors between 1792 and 1838. Its two first daughter parishes are Sainte Luce at Upper Frenchville (chapel 1826, register 1843) in the west and Saint Bruno de Grand Rivière at Van Buren in the east (chapel 1826, register 1838), both situated on the south shore of the Saint John River.

1838-1871   **Saint Basile** parish still includes both sides of the Saint John River from the Quisibis River at its east end to Ruisseau Quatre Milles (Four-Mile Brook) beyond the Madawaska River at its west end. From 1842-on, parishioners on the south side of the River are American Citizens in Aroostook County, Maine, while parishioners on the north side of the

16

River are Canadian Citizens in Madawaska County, New Brunswick. Its next daughter parish is Saint David (1871), created after all American families became part of the Diocese of Portland, Maine.

Valley East (Quisibis River to Tobique River)

1838-1868   **Saint Bruno**, the second parish in the Upper Saint John Valley, continued Saint Basile's work as a missionary church to all those living in the Greater Saint John Valley Watershed. As with Sainte Luce in the west, missions had been held there by priests from Saint Basile since 1826 when a chapel was constructed opposite Grand Rivière in today's Keegan. Initially, its borders include both sides of the Saint John River, including its tributaries, from the Quisibis in the west, at least as far as the Tobique (initially Woodstock) in the east, and all of the Aroostook River communities to the south. An examination of its registers shows that its priests visited the Indian community at Tobique, went up to logging camps on the Restigouche, and visited the Catholic Irish on the Aroostook River above Fort Fairfield. Its first two daughter parishes are Saint Léonard de Port Maurice (1868) at Parent, where services had been rendered and a separate register maintained since 1854, and Assomption (1968) at Grand Falls. These two parishes were both started as missions in 1854. Its third daughter parish is Sacré Coeur (1881), directly south along the stage coach road in North Caribou.

Valley West (Madawaska River to Saint Francis River)

1843-1859   **Sainte Luce**, the second daughter church of Saint Basile, served all of the western end of the old Madawaska Settlement, often referred to as the Upper Madawaska Settlement and, for a period of time, as the Chatauqua area. As with Saint Bruno in the east, missions had been held there by priests from Saint Basile since 1826 when a chapel was built. Situated at the mouth of Dickey Brook in Upper Frenchville, its initial boundaries included both sides of the Saint John River from Ruisseau Quatre Milles, west of the Madawaska River, all the way to the Saint Francis River. Its first daughter parish is Saint François-Xavier (1859), followed by Saint Hilaire (1868), and Sainte Agathe (1889).

1859-1871   A year before he took up residence at Sainte Luce, Fr. Dionne directed the building of a chapel at Saint François to meet the needs of families further up the river. In 1859, **Saint François-Xavier** got a resident priest and served both sides of the Saint John River from the Saint Francis River in the southwest to the Fish River in the northeast. Its daughter parishes are Saint Francis of Assisi (1889) at Claire, opposite Fort Kent, and Notre Dame du Rosaire (1950) at Connors.

Post-Ecclesial Separation: 1868/1871-1950

In the 1850s, a movement began among families in Grand Isle Township to separate parishes on the south side from those on the north. The effort generated considerable acrimony but was finally successful. In August 1870, Pius IX signed a papal degree, making all families living in Aroostook part of the Diocese of Portland, Maine. However, the ecclesial separation did not result in the movement of church records. Parish registers remained with their churches, regardless of on which side of the river a family lived.

Thus, individuals seeking entries for the baptism (birth), marriage, and burial (death) of family members must not ask, "On which side of the Saint John River did my family live?" Instead, they must ask, "Before 1868/1871 or after?" Before 1868 in the east and west, and before 1871 in the central valley, church records exist only in one of four churches: Saint François-Xavier, Sainte Luce, Saint Basile, or Saint Bruno. Researchers must find which church was closest to the family they seek to document. After 1868 in the east and west and after 1871 in the central valley, church records exist at the closest church on the side of the river that the family lived.

Valley Center: the Canadian Side (Madawaska River to Quisibis River)

In Canada, what had been part of the parish of Saint Basile eventually evolved into the civil parishes of Madawaska (1833), Saint Basile (1850), Sainte Anne (1877), and Saint Jacques (1877) . All are in Madawaska County.

1871-	**Saint Basile** now serves half the geography it had, but the growing population makes up for the change. It boundaries now extend to the Madawaska River in the west, up to the boundary with Québec in the northwest, and down to the Quisibis in the east. Its next daughter parishes are Sainte Anne (1872), at the Quisibis River, and Immaculé Conception (1880) in Edmundston.
1872-	**Sainte-Anne-de-Madawaska** is split off from Saint Basile and Saint Léonard-Parent, each parish having had responsibility for the mission for the past four years. Searchers will need to search both Saint Basile and Saint Léonard registers during this interim, since the origin of the priest determines the location of the record. The new parish serves families between the Green River to the Siegas River. Its daughter parish is Notre-Dame-de-Lourdes (1914).
1880-	**Immaculé Conception** is separated from Saint Basile to serve the growing population of Edmundston. When Madawaska County and the western-most parts of Victoria County become a separate diocese in 1944, the church will be elevated to the status of cathedral. Visitors will hear this parish church called "la Cathédral" by Valley residents. Its boundaries include the spreading town and extend as far as Ruisseau Quatre Milles in the west.
1892-	**Saint Jacques le Majeur** is separated from Immaculé Conception to serve the area along the Madawaska River toward Lake Témouiscata up to the boundary line with Québec. It had maintained its own register since 1880. Today, it is thought of as being part of Edmundston
1914-	**Notre-Dame-de-Lourdes** is separated from Sainte Anne to serve the second and third tier farm families behind Siegas as far back as the Restigouche Co. line.

1919-	**Saint Joseph** is separated from Immaculé Conception to serve the area north and east of the Madawaska River up to the Restigouche Co. line.
1923-	**Sacré-Coeur de Jésus** at Rivière Verte, a mission of Saint Basile since 1890 with its own chapel since 1910, is separated from its parent parish to serve the old, established river valley families between the parishes of Saint Basile and Sainte Anne as well as the second and third tier farm families as far back as the Restigouche Co. line. Sacré-Coeur is the final parish opened in the central valley area on the Canadian side.

Valley Center: the American Side (Madawaska River to Quisibis River)

In the United States, what had been part of the parish of Saint Basile eventually evolved into the townships or plantations of Madawaska and Saint David. Both are in Aroostook County.

1871-	When all of Maine became part of the Diocese of Portland, Maine, all of the south side of Saint Basile parish (Madawaska and Grand Isle Townships) became **Saint David** parish, and a church was built near the site of the mission that Saint Basile had served irregularly for some years. Its western boundary with Sainte Luce was at about Ruisseau Quatre Milles, about four miles west (upstream) from the mouth of the Madawaska River; its eastern boundary with Saint Bruno was opposite the mouth of the Quisibis River, where Sainte Anne de Madawaska is today. During its first ten years of existence, it was served by Fr. Sweron who lived at Sainte Luce; the parish received its first resident priest only in 1881. Its first daughter parish is Notre Dame de Mont Carmel (1880) at Lille, in the east, followed by Sainte Agathe (1889), to the south, at the top of Long Lake.
1880-	**Notre Dame de Mont Carmel** is separated from Saint David and Saint Bruno, and its partially built chapel is moved from its original location at the boundary between Grand Isle and Madawaska Townships to a new location opposite Sainte Anne, three miles upriver from Grand Isle Island. The parish serves Grand Isle Township families. It would develop a mission that would become its own parish, Saint Gerard (1930).
1889-	**Sainte Agathe** is separated from Saint David and Sainte Luce at the northern end of Long Lake. It serves the back lot families from both parishes. In turn, it will establish a daughter parish, Saint Joseph (1939) at the head of the brook connecting Long Lake with Mud Lake.
1930-	**Saint Gerard** in the village of Grand Isle is separated from Notre Dame de Mont Carmel to serve the families at the western end of Grand Isle Township.
1939-	**Saint Joseph** in Sinclair is separated from Sainte Agathe.

Valley East: the Canadian Side (Quisibis River to Salmon River)

In Canada, what had been Saint Bruno's missions eventually evolved into the civil parishes of Saint Léonard (1850), Grand Falls (1852), and Drummond (1872). When

Madawaska County was separated from Victoria County in 1873, the county line paralleled the north-south US-Canada border.

1868- Shortly before the papal edict made all American citizens part of the Diocese of Portland, Maine, Bishop Rogers of the Diocese of Chatham, New Brunswick, who had voted for the change, separated **Saint Léonard de Port Maurice** at Parent from its mother parish, Saint Bruno. A separate register had been maintained by Saint Bruno pastors at Parent since 1854, so genealogists can find entries for family members who lived on the north side of the river in Saint Léonard's register from that date. Initially, the parish's boundaries went from the Quisibis River in the west to the Tobique River in the east, but only on the north side of the Saint John River. Its service area initially included the Grand Rivière up into the Restigouche area. Its daughter parishes are Assomption (1868) at Grand Falls, Sainte Anne (1872) at Quisibis, Saint André (1903) several miles north of the Saint John River and almost in line with the eastern boundary of Maine and New Brunswick, and Saint Antoine de Padoué (1924) in the village of Saint Léonard itself.

Genealogical researchers need to keep in mind a confusing change. The name given to a general area is often that of the church serving that area. Villages near the church also often take the name of their churches. Thus Saint Léonard is the name of the civil parish and it is the name of the first church that served its residents. The name of the church is also used for the little village that grew up at the ferry crossing two miles away, just opposite the growing town of Van Buren. In time, the village was more populous and had all the civil offices as well as a larger church building serving more people. In 1946, the bishop at the time exchanged the names of the two churches. The mother church, Saint Léonard de Port Maurice in Parent, known by that name in all its records since its register was created by priests at Saint Bruno in 1854, became Saint Antoine de Padoué. And the daughter church, known as Saint Antoine de Padoué in all its records since the days that it was a mission of its mother parish at Parent, became Saint Léonard de Port Maurice. Visitors will still hear locals referring to the older, parent church as "Saint Léonard-Parent" and the younger, daughter church as "Saint Léonard-Ville." Researchers need to keep in mind the year the change was made to keep the two identities separate.

1868- When Saint Léonard was separated from Saint Bruno, so was Assomption in Grand Falls. Its initial service area went as far south as Perth-Andover and the newly developing farm areas to the east and north. Its daughter parishes are Saint Anne (1870) at Tobique First Nation, Saint Michel (1890) at Drummond to the east, Saint Joseph (1903) at Tilley to the south, and Saint André (1903) to the north and west. As the population grew further, additional parishes were separated from Assomption: Saint Thomas Aquinas (1907) at Plaster Rock, Saint Patrick (1921) at Limestone Siding, Our Lady of Mercy (1925) at Aroostook, Saint Mary of the Angels (1946) at Perth-Andover, and Saint Georges (1950) to deal with the north and east sides of the Saint John River at Grand Falls.

1890- A full generation after Assomption was staffed with a residential priest, the rich farm land to the east was populous enough to justify a parish of its own. **Saint Michel**'s service area includes the farmland outside the immediate vicinity of Grand Falls south along the Salmon River and stretching north to the Restigouche Co. line.

1903-   **Saint André** was separated from Assomption and Saint Léonard at Parent to serve the growing farm community that had developed on the back lots between the two parishes. The church was built near the former boundary separating its parent parishes.

1924-   As the town of Van Buren developed and grew on the American side in the 1890s, the village of Saint Léonard developed and grew opposite it. In time, it had a chapel served by the priest two miles to the east at Saint Léonard-Parent. In 1924, Saint Léonard-Ville it had its own priest. Its parish was called **Saint Antoine de Padoué** until 1946, when it exchanged its name with its mother parish at Parent.

1950-   **Saint Georges** was separated from Assomption to serve families living on the north and east sides of the Saint John River in the immediate vicinity of Grand Falls.

There are several other parishes within the limits of today's Diocese of Edmundston; they are not listed here since they do not serve predominantly the Acadian and French-Canadian settlers of the Upper Saint John Valley.

Valley East: the American Side (Quisibis River to Salmon River)

1871-   When Saint David was established to serve the center valley, Fr. Vallée relocated the church of **Saint Bruno** from its original location opposite the mouth of Grand Rivière (Keegan), to a point two miles to the east to better serve its far-flung parishioners and the growing village at Violette Brook (Van Buren). Priests spent the next five decades developing daughter parishes. With Saint Léonard and Assomption caring for distant locations up the Grand River as far as the Restigouche, the Salmon River, the Tobique River, Saint Bruno could concentrate on the movement of families southward and the now well developed communities in the Aroostook River Valley. Its service area extended west to Lille, east to the border, and south through the Aroostook River Valley. As each daughter parish is established, Saint Bruno relinquishes responsibility for the area served by the new parish.

1881-   The first daughter parish of Saint Bruno after ecclesial separation is **Sacré Coeur**, immediately south along the stage coach road between Van Buren on the Saint John River and Caribou on the Aroostook River. It served families who settled rich farm lands in Connors and North Caribou townships along with some families from Cyr Plantation.

1921-   **Saint Joseph**, in Hamlin, long a mission of Saint Bruno, is separated and serves families in the eastern two-thirds of Hamlin Plantation and the northern half of Caswell Plantation.

1923-   **Saint Rémi** at Keegan, built barely 200 yards from the original location of Saint Bruno, became a separate parish but remained under the

21

administration of its mother parish, Saint Bruno. This is the last parish to be established in the eastern end of the Valley on the American side of the river.

Valley West: the Canadian Side (Madawaska River to Saint Francis River)

In Canada, the area formerly served by the parishes of Sainte Luce on the American side and Saint François Xavier on the Canadian side eventually evolved into the civil parishes of Saint François (1877) and Saint Hilaire (1877).

1868- In the same year that Bishop Rogers separated Saint Léonard - Parent from Saint Bruno, he created a new parish, Saint Hilaire, and separated it from Sainte Luce. Built on land nearly opposite its mother church, its boundaries went from Ruisseau Quatre Milles to its east and up to Claire opposite Fish River in the west. Its daughter parish would be Saint Coeur de Marie (1925) in Baker Brook.

1889- **Saint François d'Assise** in Claire, opposite Fort Kent, is separated from Saint François Xavier. Although it had its own priest and its own register, it remained under the administrative direction of its mother parish. It serves the families along the Saint John River between Saint François Xavier and Saint Hilaire. Its daughter parish is Saint Thomas d'Aquin (1925) at Lac Baker.

1904- **Saint Thomas d'Aquin** at Baker Lake is separated from Saint François d'Assise. Families had been in the area since 1855, quarterly missions had been conducted since the 1860s, and a chapel had been built since 1876.

1925- **Saint Coeur de Marie** is separated from Saint Hilaire to serve the families living in the area of Baker Brook.

1938- **Notre Dame des Sept Douleurs** is separated from Immaculé Conception to serve half of Edmundston's population.

1950- **Notre Dame du Rosaire** at Connors, long a mission of Saint François Xavier, is now its own parish. It is the last parish founded in the Diocese of Edmundston in the Upper Madawaska.

Valley West: the American Side (Madawaska River to Saint Francis River)

1871- **Sainte Luce** in the west, like Saint Bruno in the east, spends the next half century developing parishes on the south side of the Saint John River. After 1871, Sainte Luce assumed responsibility for Saint Louis at Fort Kent (previously served by Saint François-Xavier) until a full-time priest became available in 1875. All its subsequent missions are in-land, outside the valley.

1872- **Saint Louis de la Décharge** was built near the mouth of the Fish River almost opposite the fort that had been built during the bloodless Aroostook War and named for an early governor of the state. From 1854 until 1871, it was a mission of Saint François Xavier, reverting to Sainte Luce after ecclesiastical separation. It did not get a full-time resident priest until 1875. Saint Louis was responsible for serving all of the

22

American side up to the mouth of the Saint Francis River where it conducted missions and established its first daughter church, Saint Charles (1891). Following that, all its missions are in-land, along the Fish River and the chain of lakes that feed it.

1891-   **Saint Charles**, initially served as a mission by Sainte Luce in the early 1850s then by Saint François Xavier, became the responsibility of Saint Louis after 1872. Situated at the mouth of the Saint Francis River, the westernmost border between Maine and New Brunswick, this parish served families along the Saint John River downstream in today's Saint Francis and Saint John Townships and upstream towards the Allagash where a chapel was built (Saint Paul, 1929). Its daughter parish is Saint John (1930).

1892-   **Saint Mary** at Eagle Lake is separated from Saint Louis to serve families between Saint Louis and Sainte Agathe.

1895-   **Saint Joseph** in Wallagrass separated from Saint Louis to serve the individuals settling along the Fish River between Fort Kent and Eagle Lake.

1906-   **Holy Family** in Daigle is separated from Saint Louis and Sainte Luce to serve the families living south of the Saint John River between Fort Kent and Frenchville.

1929-   **Saint Thomas Aquinas** is separated from Saint David to serve the growing town of Madawaska directly opposite Edmundston.

1930-   **Saint John**, a chapel serving Saint John Township families between Saint Louis and Saint Charles, finally separates from Saint Louis to became an independent parish in 1930.

1939-   **Saint Joseph** in Sinclair is separated from Sainte Agathe.

There are several other parishes within the limits of the Diocese of Portland in Aroostook County; they are not listed here since they do not serve predominantly the Acadian and French-Canadian settlers of the Upper Saint John Valley.

After 1950, outward migration and negative population change will result in church mergers and closings.

Microfilm Numbers of Parish Registers

On what is now the American side of the valley, only two Catholic churches have their registers on microfilm. Saint Bruno de Grand Rivière is available from 1838 through 1900, and Sainte Luce is available from 1843 through 1943. There is but one source for these microfimls, the Drouin Genealogical Institute. For other churches, one must depend on the **Published Marriage Repertoires** of Langlois, Voskuhl, and Guimond.

On what is now the Canadian side of the valley, most Catholic church registers plus those of Saint John the Baptist Anglican and Saint Paul's UCC are available on microfilm. There are two sources of these microfilmed church registers. One is the

Provincial Archives of New Brunswick (PANB); the other is the Church of Jesus Christ of the Latter Day Saints, the Mormons (LDS).

The following list provides the Drouin, PANB, and LDS microfilm numbers for the parishes within the scope of this monograph. The Drouin films can be purchased through its web site at www.institutdrouin.com/microfilms/MF-US.pdf. PANB films can be borrowed through and viewed at libraries participating in the inter-library loan system (both University of Maine campuses); they may also be purchased directly from the PANB. LDS films cannot be purchased but can be borrowed through and viewed at the LDS Family History Center, 67 Paris Snow Drive, Caribou ME, 207-492-4381. Additional films numbers can be found at the PANB web site, www.gnb.ca/archives/e/CountyGuides-e.asp and at the LDS web site, www.familysearch.org/Eng/Library/FHL/frameset_library.asp. The PANB collection includes most of the Catholic parishes and two Protestant parishes within Madawaska and Victoria counties, while the smaller LDS collection focuses on older parishes. The CDEM at the University of Moncton at Edmundston has a copy of most of the microfilms of Upper Saint John Valley church registers held at the PANB. Searchers may access its holdings at the CDEM web site, www.cuslm.ca/cedem/, under "Livres et Périodiques." Several public libraries on the Canadian side have some of the microfilms. Searchers may locate them by using the regional library's web site search engine at http://vision.gnb.ca. As this book was in its final stages of editing, both the Acadian Archives in Fort Kent and the CDEM in Edmundston were in the process of acquiring the Drouin microfilms of Saint Bruno's and Sainte Luce's registers.

There is a single parish not located within the Upper Saint John Valley in the list below, that of Sainte Anne de Pays Bas, located in Fredericton. It is included in this list since members of almost all its families eventually moved to the Upper Saint John Valley.

Because PANB and LDS films have been updated at different times, the dates covered by the film numbers below may not match. That is, PANB and LDS films may cover different years than those specified. When the coverage of the two differ, the dates of the PANB film are used. Drouin film numbers are identified in this list with the word "Drouin" after the number.

Readers are cautioned that registers do not always coincide with the formal establishment of a parish with its own residential priest; the register was often started before a residential priest could be assigned to the new parish. Moreover, at least with baptisms, it sometimes happened that a couple went to the closest church, regardless of what side of the river it was on, especially if they knew that the priest of the parish they belonged to was away serving a mission. Likewise, searchers should remember that, prior to 1868, Saint Bruno, Saint Basile, Sainte Luce, and Saint François Xavier served families on both sides of the river.

With the exception of Saint Paul's in Edmundston (Presbyterian then United Church) and Saint John the Baptist in Edmundston (Anglican), all the following microfilms are for Roman Catholic parishes registers.

Town / Parishes	Years	PANB	LDS
Baker-Brook/Saint-Coeur-de-Marie	1925-1951	F15754	
	1952-1993	F15755	

Town / Parishes	Years	PANB	LDS
Baker Lake/Saint-Thomas-d'Aquinas	1886-1923	F15756	859887
	1924-1993	F15757	
Clair/Saint-François-d'Assise	1889-1926	F15708	859889
	1927-1993	F15709	
Connors/Notre-Dame-du-Rosaire	1935-1993	F15705	
Drummond/Saint-Michel	1890-1920	F1434	859892
Edmundston/Immaculée-Conception	1880-1900	F15725	859890
	1900-1921	F15726	859890
	1921-1936	F15727	
	1936-1950	F15728	
	1950-1968	F15729	
	1968-1993	F15730	
Edmundston/Notre-Dame-des-7-Douleurs	1938-1993	F15732, F15733	
Edmundston/Notre-Dame de Sacré Coeur	1950-1993	F15736	
Edmundston/Saint John the Baptist Anglic	1792-1839	F1730	
	1839-1850	F1731	
Edmundston/Saint Paul (UCC)	1898-1925	F1128	
	1925-1975	F10844, F10845	
	1975-1990	F15546	
Fredericton/Sainte-Anne-des-Pays-Bas	1806-1823	F15739	
Frenchville/Sainte-Luce	1843-1852	3346 Drouin	
	1853-1916	3347 Drouin	
	1916-1943	3348 Drouin	
Grand-Falls/Assomption	1868-1920	F1435	859893
Grand-Falls/Saint-Georges	1950-1993	F15719	
Rivière-Verte/Sacré Coeur de Jésus	1938-1993	F15735	
Saint-André/Saint André	1903-1944	F15700	859891
	1944-1993	F15701	
Sainte-Anne/Sainte Anne	1886-1940	F15741	859891
	1941-1968	F15742	
	1969-1993	F15743	
Saint-Basile/Saint Basile	1767-1791	F15738	
	1792-1838	F13332	859896/7
	1838-1858	F13328	859898
	1859-1886	F13329	859899
	1887-1926	F13319	859900
	1927-1966	F13320	
	1967-1975	F13321	
	1976-1993	F15737	
Saint-François/Saint-François-Xavier	1859-1936	F15706	859895
	1937-1993	F15707	

Town / Parishes	Years	PANB	LDS
Saint-Hilaire/Saint Hilaire	1869-1894	F15745	859888
	1895-1954	F15746	
	1955-1993	F15747	
Saint-Jacques/Saint-Jacques le Majeur	1880-1907	F15720	859896
	1908-1951	F15721	
	1951-1993	F15722	
Saint Joseph/Saint Joseph	1919-1993	F15718	
Saint-Léonard-Parent/			
Saint-Antoine-de-Padoue	1854-1921	F1436	859894
	1921-1993	F15713	
Saint-Léonard-Ville/			
Saint-Léonard, Port-Maurice	1924-1950	F15710	
	1951-1993	F15712	
Seigas/Notre-Dame-de-Lourdes	1914-1993	F15744	
Van Buren/Saint Bruno	1838-1841	3135 Drouin	
	1841-1900	3136 Drouin	

Vital Records and Civil Registrations

American Side

In the United States, each township was required to maintain a record of births, marriages, and deaths beginning in 1892. At given times, townships must send a copy to the Office of Vital Statistics in Augusta.

For vital records between 1892 and 1922, individuals must write to:

Maine State Archives
84 State House Station
Augusta ME 04333-0084

Individuals should read the Frequently Asked Questions web page maintained by the Archives before making a request: www.state.me.us/sos/arc/research/vrfaqs.htm. There is a non-refundable fee for making a six-year search (includes copy if located), and individuals must provide the likely year of the event. Wise individuals will provide the information requested by the Office of Vital Records at www.state.me.us/dhs/bohodr/recorder.htm when making a request of the Archives. (Separate pages list what should be provided for births, marriages, divorces, and deaths.)

A microfilm copy of all 1892 through 1922 vital records are available at the Archives and visitors may do their own searches for free. Unfortunately, all instances of a surname throughout the state are aggregated for a given year, making searches difficult for common surnames.

Marriages between 1892 and 1966 and between 1976 and 1996 and deaths between 1960 and 1996 are searchable via the Internet. Links to search screens are available at the Archives web site, www.state.me.us/sos/arc/geneology/. Unfortunately, parents are not provided for spouses in the marriage search report, and neither parents nor spouse information is provided for death reports.

Although the state required townships to keep records starting in 1892, a few towns had already begun to do so. In the Upper Saint John River Valley, only Madawaska Township collected vital records prior to 1892. The town started in 1871, the year that ecclesial separation was implemented. In addition, Van Buren's hard working town clerk, Victorie Dufour, constructed a list of all births from Saint Bruno's register, covering the years 1838, when the register started, through 1893, a full year after the state law took effect. Dufour did not construct a list of marriages or of deaths. Both Madawaska's and Van Buren's early records are on file at the Maine State Archives and at their respective town offices. In addition, a photocopy of the Dufour index of births is available at the Acadian Archives at the University of Maine at Fort Kent and at the Abel J. Mornealt

Memorial Library in Van Buren. It is also available on microfilm (number FHL US/CAN film 12275) with the title, "Index of the birth records 1838-1893,included, copied from the authentic registers of St. Bruno's Parish, Van Buren, Maine" in the LDS microfilm collection.

For events that took place between 1923 and the present, individuals must write to:

Office of Vital Records
Human Services Building
221 State Street
Augusta ME 04333-0011

Requests must be accompanied by the information required by the Office and listed at its web site, www.state.me.us/dhs/bohodr/recorder.htm. There is a separate list for births, marriages, divorces, and deaths. A check must accompany the request. Requests may be made through an automated telephone system with a credit card at 1-877-523-2659.

The same records available at the Office of Vital Records and at the Maine State Archives are also available in each township. Searchers may write to a township to request a copy of a record. A fee is charged which varies by township. Searchers should know that clerks for smaller townships have other, full-time jobs. The following is a list of town clerks with phone numbers and mailing addresses as of June 2002.

Allagash

Nola Begin
Phone: 207-398-3198
RR 1 Box 146
Allagash ME 04774

Caswell

Paula Peers
Phone: 207-325-4604
1020 Van Buren Road
Limestone ME 04750

Cyr Plantation

Janet Lapierre
Phone: 728-3802
HCR 63 Box 64B
Cyr Plantation
Van Buren ME 04785

Eagle Lake

James Nadeau
Phone: 207-444-5125
RR1, Box 2338
Eagle Lake ME 04739

Fort Kent

Rella J. Dubois
Phone: 207-834-3090
416 West Main Street
Fort Kent ME 04743

Frenchville

Philip G. Levesque
Phone: 207-543-7301
P.O. Box 97, 283
US Route 1
Frenchville ME 04745

Grand Isle

Helene M. Sirois
Phone: 207-895-3420
P.O. Box 197, 317 Main Street
Grand Isle ME 04746

Hamlin

William H. Parent
Phone: 207-868-2740
HCR 62, Box 33
Van Buren ME 04785

Madawaska

Arthur Faucher
Phone: 207-728-6351
328 St. Thomas Street, Suite 101
Madawaska ME 04756

Madawaska Lake Twp.

Roland D. Martin
Phone: 493-3318
144 Sweden Street, Suite #1
Caribou ME 04736

New Canada

Rodney Pelletier
Phone: 207-834-4004
27 Thibeault Road
New Canada ME 04743

Saint Agatha

Ryan Pelletier
Phone: 207-543-7305
P.O. Box 110, 419 Main Street
St. Agatha ME 04772

Sinclair Twp.

Ryan Pelletier
Phone: 207-543-7305
P.O. Box 110, 419 Main Street
St. Agatha ME 04772

St. Francis

Claudette Michaud
Phone: 207-398-3175
P.O. Box 98, R1 Main Road
St. Francis ME 04774

St. John Plantation

Joyce Martin
Phone: 207-834-6444
1825 St. John Road
St. John Plantation ME 04743

Un. Twp. of T17 R5

Ryan Pelletier
Phone: 543-7305
P.O. Box 110, 419 Main Street
St. Agatha ME 04772

Van Buren

Kathleen L. Cyr
Phone: 207-868-2886
65 Main Street
Van Buren ME 04785

Wallagrass

Bonnie Lamarre
Phone: 207-834-2263
P.O. Box 10
Wallagrass ME 04781

Canadian Side

Civil registrations of births, marriages, and deaths have been kept in New
Brunswick since 1886. However, county returns are so spotty until 1920 as to make a
search not worth the effort. Moreover, neither Madawaska nor Victoria County returned

any record between 1901 and 1920. Returns from 1920 until 1952 are complete. Due to privacy laws, records for events after 1952 are not available to the public. Civil registrations are an especially rich source of data. Death records, for instance, include the name of the deceased, how long the person lived in New Brunswick, birth date, names of parents, name of spouse, cause of death, and the name of the person providing the information.

Three-year searches of records will be conducted by provincial staff upon receipt of a fee provided that the full name of the party, approximate date, and place of event are given with the request. Requests must be mailed to:

Vital Statistics Branch
Department of Health and Community Services
P. O. Box 6000
Fredericton New Brunswick E3B 5H1

Individuals may also visit Vital Statistics Branch at:

Vital Statistics Branch
Department of Health and Community Services
City Centre, Room 203
435 King Street
Fredericton New Brunswick E3B 1E5

A description of services provided to genealogists and fees required are given the New Brunswick Health and Wellness web site at www.gnb.ca/0379/en/services.htm.

The same information available at the Vital Statistics Branch can be interlibrary loaned from:

Provincial Archives
Supply and Services
P. O. Box 6000
Fredericton New Brunswick E4B 5H1

Microfilm numbers for given years are listed in the County Finding Aid for Madawaska and for Victoria Counties at the Archives web site, www.archives.gnb.ca/Archives/EN/CountyGuides-e.aspx.

Published Marriage Repertories

Many individuals have been at this business of finding out who our ancestors are for some time. Some of them have printed their work, and eight of them are listed here. With a single exception, these books are lists of marriages which occurred in a Catholic church and in which at least one of the partners was a practicing Catholic. The one exception, the Poitras répertoire contains marriages which occurred at Saint John the Baptist Anglican church and at Saint Paul UCC, both in Edmundston. Individuals who research Protestant families must turn to the vital records kept by New Brunswick beginning in 1886 and by Maine beginning in 1893. Those are described in the Vital Records and Civil Registrations section above.

The works in this list are divided into three groupings. The first includes repertoires of marriages that occurred in the Upper Saint John Valley. Those repertoires cover the time period from 1792 through to the 1920s or later depending on the repertory. The second grouping includes repertoires of marriages that occurred in the Bas Saint Laurent region. Most French-Canadians who moved to the Valley from Québec came from there. The third grouping is made up of two works that are not repertoires but genealogies. In them, searchers will find marriages of individuals between the mid-1600s through to 1755 and a little beyond. By using works from all three groupings, searchers can trace both Acadian and French-Canadian family members back to the mid 17th century. Searchers whose family members were non-Catholic Yankees, Loyalists, Irish, or Scots will need to turn to other resources at the Maine State Archives and at the Provincial Archives of New Brunswick described in the Melnyk and the Punch and Sanborn books described in the Related Resource Publications section later in the monograph.

Searchers who use these published marriage repertoires must keep in mind that it is all too easy to make a mistake when copying a record. Searchers should seek other records to confirm what they find in published repertoires.

An important caveat must be mentioned regarding the identity of parents for Catholic marriages that occurred between 1872 and 1893 in Canadian-side churches and between 1859 and 1900 in American-side churches served by Fr. Sweron. The names supplied in Langlois/Lang are some times the best guesses of the families Fr. Langlois consulted. In some cases, the information he received was correct. In many cases, the information he received was incorrect. In the Voskuhl enhancement of Langlois/Lang, some of the initial guesses have been corrected by recent family researchers, but many errors remain. Searchers using the Langlois/Lang or Voskuhl compilations should carefully evaluate information they take from those works for the dates mentioned above. Only in the Poitras compilation is every single name justified by an official document, either a church register entry or a civil marriage or death certificate on file at the Maine State Archives or Provincial Archives of New Brunswick. Where Poitras could not get the identity of the parents from an official document, he left the space blank.

All of the repertoires listed below are among the holdings of the two archives in the Valley; many are in the holdings of the public libraries on both sides of the Valley.

Repertoires of Valley Marriages

Langlois, Henri, comp. and Ernest Lang, ed. *Dictionnaire Généalogique du Madawaska: Repertoire des Mariages des Paroises de la Vallée Superieure de la Rivière Saint Jean au Nouveau Brunswick (La région indiquée ci-haut comprend le diocèse d'Edmundston, ainsi que le comté d'Aroostook-Maine).* Saint Basile de Madawaska, New Brunswick: n.p., 1971.

This multi-volume compilation includes marriages performed in Roman Catholic churches on both sides of the Upper Saint John Valley. Thus, it includes Madawaska County, New Brunswick (1792-1935) and Aroostook County, Maine (1792-1920). Although the vast majority of entries are marriages performed in the Valley, the listing includes many marriages performed outside the Valley in Canada, enabling Valley residents of French-Canadian origin to trace their ancestry back to Québec. Fr. Langlois made the compilation between 1962 and 1967 while he was chaplain at the Fort Kent People's Benevolent Hospital. After he died, his friend, Fr. Lang, of the Diocese of Edmundston, saw his work through to publication. Readers need to be suspicious of any entry which identifies the parents for marriages between 1872 and 1893 in a church on the Canadian side and for marriages between 1859 and 1900 in a church served by Fr. Sweron on the American side. Family members that Fr. Langlois contacted supplied correct information in some cases; in others they are incorrect guesses. In addition, Fr. Langlois began his work as an effort to trace several family lines. Although he later attempted to become comprehensive, there are a number of marriages that took place in . The Valley which are not included in this work. Users will find some entries in incorrect alphabetical order. (Example: Madore is found after Leclerc and before Lecourt.) Likewise, users will find entries for families with name variations grouped together. (Example: entries for Boniface-Roy, Roy, Desjardins, and Lauzier are all in the R section.) These two practices make the work harder to use. The Langlois/Lang repertory and the Voskuhl enhancement of it are the only two repertories of Valley marriages to include some of those which occurred on the south side of the valley after the ecclesial separation described in the Church Registers section above. A copy is available at many valley libraries. A reprint is available for purchase in four volumes under the title, Genealogies of the Catholic Families of Aroostook County, Maine and the Catholic Diocese of Edmundston, New Brunswick, at Quintin Publications, 22 Delta Drive, Pawtucket, RI 02860-4555, www.quintinpublications.com, 401-723-6797.

Voskuhl, Diane P. LaVerdière, and Robert K. Voskuhl. *Genealogies of the Catholic Families of Maine, New Brunswick, and the Province of Québec.* Norfolk, Va.: D.P.L. Voskuhl and R.K. Voskuhl, 1999.

This six-volume compilation is an enhancement of Langlois/Lang DGM. To the original retyped Langlois/Lang compilation, the Voskuhls added a number of the marriages which occurred on the American side and many marriages from some 21 compilations covering old Québec City and the towns and counties of the lower Saint Lawrence from which many families came to the Upper Saint John Valley. The multi-volume compilation comes in two parts, the first alphabetized by male names, the second alphabetized by female names. The Voskuhls' major improvement over Langlois/Lang is their complete realphabetization of entries, their listing by brides as well as by grooms, and their loading the entire list onto a searchable CD which costs a small fraction of the paper version. Because the compilers continue to accept corrections from genealogists, they have been able to correct some of the original errors in Langlois / Lang; others remain. A copy (paper or CD) can also be purchased from the compilers at 8220 Halprin Drive, Norfolk VA 23518, 757-583-1053.

> Poitras, Jean-Guy, comp. *Répertoire des mariages au Nord-Ouest du Nouveau-Brunswick, Canada, pour les Comtés de Madawaska, Restigouche (partiellement) et Victoria, 1792-2001.* Edmundston, New Brunswick: Jean-Guy Poitras, 2002.

Published in the summer of 2002, this work gets its information directly from church registers as augmented by official birth, marriage, and death certificates on file at the Provincial Archives of New Brunswick. The compiler has paid an aide to look up a sample of entries to confirm the accuracy of the whole. By far, it is the most accurate and comprehensive compilation of valley marriages to date. Its only weakness is that it does not include marriages of valley residents who lived on the south side of the river at the eastern end (Saint Bruno) after 1838, on the south side of the river at the western end (Sainte Luce) after 1843 or on the south side of the river in the central part of the valley (Saint David) after 1871. In addition, families living on the north side of the river at the east end (Saint Bruno) are not included between 1838 and 1854 since they are in Saint Bruno's register, and families living on the north side of the river at the west end (Sainte-Luce) are not included between 1843 and 1870 since they are in Sainte Luce's register. The compilation includes all marriages performed within Madawaska and Victoria Counties plus some of those performed in Restigouche County. It is the only compilation to include some non-Catholic marriages. Marriages are included into the 2002 year if they are recorded in church registers; however, marriages recorded only with civil authorities stop with the 1952 year due to New Brunswick's 50-year waiting rule for the public release of civil marriage data. A copy can be purchased from the author by mail at 100 34th Avenue, Edmundston NB E3V 2T5, or by fax at 506-737-5373.

Léon Guimond of Frenchville has gained permission to make extracts of marriage entries in the registers of all Catholic parishes serving predominantly Acadian and French-Canadian families in northern Aroostook County. His extracts of Sainte Luce were not made from the original register, and users have discovered the list to have many errors. Several of his compilations have been privately printed but have very limited distribution within their local area. Visitors to the area will find all of them at the Madawaska Public Library. The compiler is willing to answer questions at P.O. Box 148, Frenchville ME 04745, 207-543-6306.

Repertoires of Québec Marriages

> Roy, Jean-Guy and Michel Beaulieu, comp. *Répertoire des mariages, comté de Kamouraska, 1685-1990.* Sainte-Foy, Quebec: Société de Généalogie de Québec, 1993.

This volume is the aggregation of the extracts that Fr. Roy had started doing of each separate church parish in the County, starting with the mother churche of the area, Saint

Louis, in the town of Kamouraska. The volume contains the extracts of marriages from all Catholic church parishes in the county. Many Upper Saint John River Valley families have ancestors who married at Saint-Louis-de-Kamouraska, at Sainte-Anne-de-la-Pocatière, or at other churches in the Bas Saint Laurent area of Québec prior to settling in the Valley. The oldest parish in Kamouraska County, Saint Louis, started its register in 1685. The book is available for sale at the Société de Généalogie de Québec, Case Postal 9066, Sainte-Foy QC G1V 4A8, 418-651-9127, sgq@total.net, www.genealogie.org/club/sgq/. (Click on "Publications" then on "Publications en vente").

> Gingras, Robert-Edmond; Jean-Guy Roy, and Michel Beaulieu, comp.
> *Répertoire des Mariages Série Rivière-du-Loup et Témiscouata*. Sainte-Foy,
> Quebec: Société de Généalogie de Québec, 1988-1991.

This four-volume set contains the extracts of marriages from all Catholic church parishes in Rivière-du-Loup, Les Basques, and Témiscouata Counties in Québec. The three counties adjoin New Brunswick, and Rivière-du-Loup County straddles the old portage from Lake Témouiscata to the Saint Lawrence River. Today's Trans-Canada highway parallels that old portage. A companion to Roy's compilation of Kamouraska County marriages, the Gingras-Roy-Beaulieu work will help Upper Saint John Valley families locate ancestors who married in the Bas Saint Laurent region of Québec prior to moving to the Valley. The oldest parish in Rivière-du-Loup County, Isle-Verte, began its register in 1766; the oldest parish in Les Basques County, Notre-Dame-des-Neiges, began its register in 1713; the oldest parish in Témiscouata, Notre-Dame-du-Lac, began its register in 1861. This work represents a commitment by the publisher to interfile female names with male names. (Note that the Société de Généalogie de Québec sells each volume separately since each volume contains separate clusters of parishes.)

Acadian Genealogies

> White, Stephen A. *Dictionnaire Généalogique des Familles Acadiennes*.
> Moncton, New Brunswick: Centre d'Études Acadiennes et Université de
> Moncton, 1999.

This two volume work constitutes Part I of a larger work and covers all individuals who lived in or married someone who lived in what was known as Acadia between 1636 and 1714. White is at work on additional volumes. An English Supplement was published in 2000 which translates all introductory material, including the extensive bibliography, and all notes from within the genealogy proper. This carefully done and definitive work identifies all Acadian families. Where documentation is not clear, White discusses the available evidence and supplies readers with full references to source material. Where documents supply the information, he supplies a person's location of origin in France.

> Arsenault, Bona. *Histoire et généalogie des Acadiens*. Rev. ed.
> Québec: Leméac, 1978.

The first volume is the history. The remaining 5 volumes are the genealogy. Although written in French, the 1994 English translation of the History section has a list of words in the back that readers can use to extract everything they wish from the genealogy section of this work. Arsenault traces the founding families of Acadia from the beginning (1636) through the deportation period (to about 1768). As might be expected of a one-person effort this large, it contains errors, and searchers will want to seek confirmation of what they find here. Users of this work will want to have handy Phoebe Chauvin Morrison's *Index to Bona Arsenault's "Histoire et généalogie des Acadiens"* (Houma, La., 1990) handy to locate individuals within Arsenault's work, which is not indexed. Readers of Arsenault will also want use Janet Jehn's *Corrections & Additions to Arsenault's Histoire et généalogie des Acadiens* (Covington, Ky., 1988) and Don Boudreaux's *Discrepancies within Bona Arsenault's Histoire et généalogie des Acadiens* (Lafayette, La.: Lafayette Genealogical Society, 1966), both of which identify errors that call for additional research.

Cemeteries

One of the near-primary official documents for a person's death is his or her headstone, and for headstones, one must turn to the cemeteries. However, there are three limitations one must keep in mind. The first limitation has to do with the effects of time. Prior to the 1880's almost all headstones were carved on a single two-foot-wide wooden board. After 100 to 200 years of assault by nature's wind and sun, rain and snow, and by man's hand scythes and motorized lawn mowers, few are left standing. Almost all the ones that still stand are unreadable. Thus, as a general principle, searchers should not expect to locate a headstone prior to 1890. But even later stones, especially those made from concrete poured in to a mold, have also deteriorated due to the elements. Some have broken and distant descendants, many long gone from the area—have not replaced them. In addition, a care taker here and there has thrown away broken stones rather than seeking someone to repair them. In a few cases, the renovation of the church or the coming of the railroad resulted in graves being dug up and the remains reburied in a mass grave. Because many of these early grave markers are no longer standing and others are no longer legible, the only evidence of where an ancestor is buried is the church register or the civil death certificate.

A second limitation has to do with the accuracy of headstone data. They sometimes have errors in the spelling of the name or in the date. And in recent years, several individuals may be buried in a plot but the headstone may only identify the most recently buried person. Thus, searchers should seek other data to confirm what they find on headstones.

A third limitation is that individuals may not be buried in the parish where they were known to live for the majority of their adult lives. A couple who married and lived in Sainte Anne de Madawaska parish, for example, may have lived their final years with a son across the river and be buried at Saint Gerard Cemetery in Grand Isle Township. The reverse is true. A couple who married at Notre Dame de Mont Carmel in Lille may have lived their final years with a daughter across the river and be buried at Sainte Anne de Madawaska. Moreover, many individuals who grew up and married in the Upper Saint John Valley are buried in other states and provinces of the United States and Canada, especially from 1940-on, depending on where they moved for work or retired.

The following are the cemeteries within the Upper Saint John Valley. The majority are Catholic church cemeteries; non-Catholic cemeteries are identified in their name. As a general rule, any cemetery with the word "Saint" in its name is Catholic, while all others are non-denominational, municipal, or belong to a denomination that I have made part of the name. The organization of the following list is first by side: American or Canadian. American cemeteries are then organized alphabetically by township, while Canadian cemeteries are then organized alphabetically by civil parish. (Due to the changes in civil units of New Brunswick in the 1960s and again in the 1990s, the civil parishes used are those in effect as of the year 1900.)

In most cases, burials started in a cemetery at about the time that a chapel was built but before the church became a canonical parish.

Thanks go to author Guy Dubay of Madawaska for testing many of the directions and for making recommended changes to the listings which follow. He drove to almost all the cemeteries on the south side of the Valley and to several on the north. He measured distances to cemeteries from Van Buren to Saint John Township, from Fort Kent to Eagle Lake, and from Clair to Edmundston. Thanks are also due to Norma Kennedy Plourde for measuring distances to cemeteries located between Baker Lake and Edmundston on the north side of the Valley and to Jean-Guy Poitras for measuring the distance to Saint Joseph de Madawaska.

American Side

Allagash

Allagash Baptist Cemetery, Allagash

The cemetery is behind the church on the southeast side of ME-161, 31.4 miles west from the traffic light at the intersection of Pleasant and Main Streets (ME-11 and ME-161) in Fort Kent.

Allagash Municipal Cemetery, Allagash

The cemetery is immediately southwest of the US Forest Service station on northwest side of ME-161, 29.0 miles west from the traffic light at the intersection of Pleasant and Main Streets (ME-11 and ME-161) in Fort Kent. This cemetery was once called the Bolton Point Cemetery.

Saint Paul Catholic Cemetery, Allagash

The cemetery is opposite the church on the northwest side of ME-161, 30.4 miles west on ME-161 from the traffic light at the intersection of Pleasant and Main Streets (ME-11 and ME-161) in Fort Kent.

Saint Paul UCC Cemetery, Allagash

The cemetery is behind the church on the northwest side of ME-161, 15.8 miles west from the traffic light at the intersection of Pleasant and Main Streets (ME-11 and ME-161) in Fort Kent.

Eagle Lake

Saint Mary Cemetery, Eagle Lake

The cemetery is behind the church on the west side of ME-11, 16.7 miles south of the intersection of US-1 and ME-11 in Fort Kent.

Fort Kent

Christ Church Cemetery, Fort Kent

From the junction of Main and Pleasant Streets (ME-11 and ME-161), go south on ME-11, Pleasant Street, for 0.2 miles. The cemetery is on the east side of the street just before the entrance of the University of Maine at Fort Kent.

Saint Louis Cemetery, Fort Kent

The old cemetery is opposite the church on the south side of US-1 immediately east of the Fish River. The new cemetery is on the west side of the hospital on north side of US-1, 0.7 miles east of Saint Louis church.

Frenchville

Sainte Luce Cemetery, Upper Frenchville

The cemetery is on the east side of the church on the south side of US-1, 0.7 miles west of the Frenchville post office building on US-1.

Grand Isle Plantation

Notre Dame de Mont Carmel Cemetery, Lille

The cemetery is behind the church, in the village of Lille, on the south side of US-1, 12.1 miles west of Saint Bruno church in Van Buren.

Saint Gerard Cemetery, Grand Isle

From Madawaska, the cemetery is 1.1 miles east of the church of Saint Gerard on the south side of US-1. (It is well outside the village of Grand Isle.) From Van Buren, the cemetery is 1.9 miles west of Notre Dame de Mont Carmel church in Lille.

Hamlin Plantation

Saint Joseph Cemetery, Hamlin

The cemetery is behind the church on the south side of Alt. US-1, 1.5 miles northwest of the Caswell-Hamlin township line as you enter the valley from Limestone.

Madawaska

Saint David Cemetery, Madawaska

The cemetery is opposite the church on the south side of US-1, 2.5 miles east of the junction of Bridge Street and US-1 in the town of Madawaska.

Saint Thomas Aquinas Cemetery, Madawaska

The cemetery is on the north side of US-1 (Main Street), 0.5 mile west of the junction of Bridge Street and US-1 in the town of Madawaska.

New Canada

Holy Family Cemetery, Daigle

From the junction of US-1 and ME-161 in Fort Kent, go southeast on ME-161 for 8.8 miles to Daigle Pond. (A marker for the former church, now torn down, is on the west side of the road at that point.) Turn east at the south end of Daigle Pond onto Cemetery Hill Road for 0.2 miles. The cemetery is on the south side of the road.

North Caribou

Sacré Coeur, North Caribou

The cemetery is on the south side of the church on the east side of US-1, 4.6 miles north of the blinking light at the intersection of old US-1 and the current US-1-Bypass at Caribou.

Sainte Agatha

Sainte Agatha Cemetery, Sainte Agatha

The old cemetery is on the north side of the church on the east side of ME-162, 4.5 miles south of the junction of ME-162 and US-1 at Frenchville. The new cemetery is 0.7 miles further south on ME-162 on the west side of the road.

Saint Francis

Saint Charles Cemetery, Saint Francis

The old cemetery is on the south side of the church on the southeast side of ME-161 in Saint Francis, 17.0 miles west from the traffic light at the intersection of Pleasant and Main Streets (ME-11 and ME-161) in Fort Kent. The new cemetery is 2.1 miles northeast of the church (towards Fort Kent) on the southeast side of ME-161. The new cemetery is set back about 100 yards from the road and is easy to miss.

Saint John

Saint John Cemetery, Saint John

The cemetery is behind the church on the northwest side of ME-161, 9.0 miles west from the traffic light at the intersection of Pleasant and Main Streets (ME-11 and ME-161) in Fort Kent.

Saint John Bible Cemetery, Saint John

The cemetery is on northwest side of ME-161, 11.5 miles west from the traffic light at the intersection of Pleasant and Main Streets (ME-11 and ME-161) in Fort Kent.

Sinclair

Saint Joseph Cemetery, Sinclair

From the junction of ME-162 and US-1 in Frenchville, go south on ME-162 for 7.8 miles (3.3 miles past the church of Sainte Agathe) to the village of Sinclair. Turn left onto a wooden bridge crossing the brook connecting Long Lake to Mud Lake. The cemetery is on the left 0.5 miles from the turn onto the bridge.

T17–R5

Saint Euthrope, Guerette

The cemetery is on the southwest side of ME-162, 1.0 mile south of the junction of ME-162 and ME-161 and 18.0 miles south of the junction of ME-162 and US-1 in Frenchville.

Van Buren

Saint Bruno Cemetery, Van Buren

The cemetery is behind the church on the north side of US-1, 0.3 mile west of Violet Brook on the west side of downtown Van Buren and 0.8 mile west of the intersection of US-1 and Alt. US-1 at the east end of downtown Van Buren. Saint Bruno Cemetery served as the cemetery for Saint Rémi parish in Keegan. (Bodies at the original 1837-1871 cemetery on the north side of the road in Keegan were disinterred and reburied at this location in 1871.)

Grande Rivière Cemetery, Van Buren

The cemetery is on the east side of US-1 (Caribou Road) at the very lip of the Valley, 0.7 mile from the base of the hill and the intersection of US-1 and Alt. US-1 (Hamlin Road).

Wallagrass Plantation

Saint Joseph Cemetery, Wallagrass

The old cemetery is on the southwest side of ME-11, 10 miles south of Fort Kent in the village of Wallagrass. (The church has been torn down.) The new cemetery is another 500 feet south of the old cemetery on ME-11 behind the rectory on the northeast side of ME-11 some 500 feet away from the road.

Sacred Heart Cemetery, Soldier Pond

The cemetery behind Saint Joseph's (formerly Sacred Heart) church on ME-11 in Soldier Pond, 8.0 miles south of Fort Kent.

Canadian Side

For those who did not grow up in the Valley, the road numbers may be confusing. The major artery on the north side of the river is the Transcanada-2. It has replaced the old river road which still exists in sections. From Edmundston to past Saint Léonard, the old river road is NB-144. Whenever it is goes through a village, it is named Rue Principal. In the descriptions below, the old river road, NB-144, and Rue Principal all refer to the same thing.

Drummond

Saint Michel Cemetery, Drummond

The cemetery is opposite the church on the southwest side of NB-108, the Tobique Road, 2.5 miles southeast from the stop light at the junction of NB-130 and NB-218 at the northeast side of the bridge over the Saint John River in Grand Falls.

Grand Falls

Assomption Cemetery, Grand Sault

From the stop light at the intersection of NB-2 and Broadway Boulevard in Grand Falls, go northeast on Broadway to the first street on the right, Pleasant Street, then go two blocks to the end of the street. The old cemetery is on the west side of the church at the junction of Pleasant and Chapel Streets. The new cemetery is on the west side of NB-218, Portage Road, 0.8 miles south from the stop light at the intersection of NB-2 and Broadway Boulevard in Grand Falls.

Union Cemetery, Grand Falls

From the stop light at the northeast side of the bridge over the Saint John River, the junction of NB-130 and NB-218, cross the bridge to Grand Falls and onto Broadway Boulevard. Turn left at the first intersection, Victoria Street, and go 0.3 miles to the end of Victoria Street. The cemetery is at the junction of Victoria and Manse Streets.

Pine Hill Cemetery, Grand Falls

The cemetery is on the west side of and at the end of Broadway Boulevard, 0.2 miles southwest of the stop light at the intersection of NB-2 and Broadway Boulevard in Grand Falls.

Saint Georges Cemetery, Grand Sault

From the stop light at the northeast side of the bridge over the Saint John River, the junction of NB-130 and NB-218, go west towards Saint Léonard about six car lengths, then turn North onto Burgess Street. Go north on Burgess, which quickly becomes Resevoir Street, for 0.3 miles and turn west at Morin Street. The cemetery is set back about 50 yards off Resevoir Street.

Madawaska

Saint Joseph Cemetery, Saint Joseph

From the Transcanada, take exit 18 south on Boulevard Hébert for 0.1 mile to the first stop light. Turn west onto Monseingeur Pinchette and go 1.5 miles to the second stop light on that street. Turn northwest onto Victoria Street and go 1.0 mile to Olivier Boucher. Turn east and go 4.0 miles to Chemin Toussaint. Turn north and go 2.1 miles. The cemetery is on the south side of the church, on the west side of Chemin Toussaint.

Immaculé Conception Cemetery, Edmundston

The cemetery is on the northwest side of Rue Saint François (NB-120) 0.8 miles from the Canadian Customs house at the international bridge.

Union Cemetery, Edmundston

The cemetery is adjacent to Immaculé Conception Cemetery on the northwest side of Rue Saint François (NB-120). (Visitors will mistake it for part of Immaculé Conception Cemetery. The two are distinguished by the directions their headstones face. Immaculé Conception's part is closest to the international bridge; the Union Cemetery part is furthest from the international bridge. The two cemeteries occupy 0.2 miles of space.)

Saint John the Baptist Anglican Cemetery, Edmundston

Next to Saint John the Baptiste Anglican Church at the intersection of Rue de l'Église and Costigan Street in downtown Edmundston.

Notre Dame des Sept Douleurs Cemetery, Edmundston

From the Transcanada, take the Boulevard Hébert exit south to the first stop light, thence west on Monseigneur Pinchette for 1.5 miles to Victoria Street. The cemetery is on the north side of the intersection of Victoria Street, Mgr. Pinchette, and Boulevard Acadie.

Sainte Anne

Notre Dame de Lourdes Cemetery, Seigas

The cemetery is behind the church on the east side of the road, 2.2 miles north from the Siegas exit of the Transcanada just west of Saint Léonard and 3.4 miles north from the old river road, NB-144.

Sainte Anne Cemetery, Sainte Anne

There are four Sainte Anne cemeteries. The first and oldest is on the west side of the church surrounded by a cyclone fence. No markers survive. The headstones in the back of that cemetery are those removed from the second cemetery when the railroad cut through it. The second or "old" cemetery is off Rue Principal, 0.2 miles west of the church; the entrance on the south side of the street is very narrow and easy to miss, between a business (#148) and a private residence (#146). The cemetery is about 50 yards from the street. The third or "new" cemetery is on the south side of Rue Principal, 0.5 miles east of the church. To get to the fourth or "newest" cemetery, go west on Rue Principal 0.2 miles from the church; turn north onto Saint André for 0.3 miles, then turn west onto First Avenue. The entrance to the cemetery is 0.1 mile off Saint André and is on the north side of First Avenue.

Sacré Coeur de Jésus Cemetery, Rivière Verte

The cemetery is behind the church on the north side of NB-144, Rue Principal, 7.4 miles west of the church of Sainte Anne.

Saint Basile

Saint Basile Cemetery, Saint Basile

The cemetery is opposite the church on the south side of NB-144, Rue Principal, 1.9 miles west from the exit off the Transcanada at the east side of Saint Basile.

Saint François

. *Saint Coeur de Marie Cemetery, Baker Brook*

The cemetery is on the southeast side of NB-120, 0.4 miles northeast of the church and 4.0 miles northeast from the junction of NB-161 and NB-120.

Saint François d'Assise Cemetery, Claire

The cemetery is on the southeast side of NB-161, 0.2 miles northeast of the church and 2.1 miles northeast from the Canadian Customs house at the Fort Kent–Clair international bridge.

Saint Thomas d'Aquin Cemetery, Baker Lake

From the junction of NB-161 and NB-120, go northwest on NB-120 for 3.1 miles to Rue d'Église, thence right to cross over the railroad overpass, thence right again onto Chemin de la Pointe for 0.3 miles. The cemetery is on the right.

Saint François-Xavier Cemetery, Saint François

From the Canadian Customs house in Clair, go southwest 4.9 miles on NB-205 to the church. To get to the old cemetery, go past the church 0.1 mile, turn left onto Rue Bellevue and almost immediately right just before the Monseigneur Plourde Library. The cemetery is behind and to the left of the Ecole Ernest Lang playground. To get to the new cemetery, turn northwest in front of the church onto NB-215, Lac Unique Road, for 0.3 miles. The cemetery is on the right of the road.

45

Saint Francis Baptist Cemetery, Saint François

The cemetery is on the southwest side of the church on the northwest side of NB-205. 9.6 miles southwest of the Canadian Customs house in Clair. It is 4.7 miles southwest from Saint François-Xavier church.

Connors Memorial Cemetery, Connors

The cemetery is on the north side of the chapel on the east side of NB-205, 11.6 miles southwest from the Canadian Customs house in Clair. It is 6.7 miles southwest from Saint François-Xavier church and 0.2 miles shy of the museum store which is also on the east side of NB-205.

Notre Dame du Rosaire Cemetery, Connors

The cemetery is opposite the church on the east side of NB-205, 12.3 miles southwest from the Canadian Customs house in Clair.

Saint Hilaire

Saint Hilaire Cemetery, Saint Hilaire

The cemetery is on the northwest side of NB-120, 2.3 miles southwest of the church and 7.4 miles northeast of the junction of NB-161 and NB-120.

Saint Jacques

Saint Jacques le Majeur Cemetery, Saint Jacques

The old cemetery is next to the church on Rue Principal (Chemin Canada, NB-144) 2.5 miles northwest from the Saint Jacques exit off the Transcanada. The new cemetery is the first left (north) to the northwest of the church and the last left (northwest) turn before the bridge crossing the Madawaska River.

Saint Léonard

Saint Antoine de Padoué Cemetery. Saint Léonard-Parent

The cemetery is on the west side of the church and behind the former rectory on the north side of NB-144, 1.4 miles east of the blinking light at the intersection of rue to Pont and NB-144 (rue Principal) in Saint Léonard. (From its foundation as an independent parish in 1868 until 1946, this was the cemetery of Saint Léonard de Port Maurice.)

Protestant Cemetery, Saint Léonard-Ville

This cemetery is on the south side of rue Principal, 0.6 miles west of the blinking light at the intersection of rue du Pont and NB-144 in Saint Léonard. It is set back from the road and next to a house, and only three stones survive. It was the cemetery for Protestants who once lived in the area.

Saint Léonard de Port Maurice Cemetery, Saint Léonard-Ville

The cemetery is on the south side of NB-144, 0.6 miles west of the intersection of rue du Pont and NB-144 in Saint Léonard. The cemetery is set back at least 50 yards from the street.(From its foundation as an independent parish in 1921 until 1946, this was the cemetery of Saint Antoine de Padoué.)

Grand River United Cemetery, Saint Léonard

From the blinking light at the intersection of rue du Pont and NB-144 in Saint Léonard, go west 1.6 miles to Chemin Grand Rivière. Turn North onto that road for 1.0 mile (passing under the Transcanada), then west for another 2.3 miles. The cemetery is on the west side of the little church on the south side of Chemin Grand Rivière.

Saint André Cemetery, Saint André

From the traffic light at the northeast end of the bridge over the Saint John River in Grand Falls, go west from Grand Sault on NB-108, the Madawaska Road, for 1.7 miles. Turn north on NB-255 and go north 2.4 miles to Rue d'Église. Turn west on Rue d'Église for 0.3 miles. The cemetery is immediately behind the church on the north side of Rue d'Église; access is on the east side of the church.

Saint Eloi Cemetery, Saint André

From the traffic light at the northeast end of the bridge over the Saint John River in Grand Falls, go west from Grand Sault on NB-108, the Madawaska Road, for 1.7 miles. Turn north on NB-255 and go north 2.4 miles to Rue d'Église. Turn east and drive 2.4 miles to Chemin Montagne à Commeau, thence north 3.2 miles to the chapel. The cemetery is behind the chapel on the west side of the road; access is on the south side of the chapel. Saint Eloi is part of the parish of Saint André.

Census Returns

American Censuses

The United States took a census in 1790 and has conducted one every ten years since. The first year in which US census takers made it to the Madawaska Settlement is 1820. Since Aroostook County was not created until 1838, the 1820 and 1930 returns for communities along the Saint John River are in the returns for Penobscot County. All other returns since are in Aroostook County's returns. The 1890 census was lost to fire. The last census released to the public is the 1930 return. Each return for Aroostook County is organized by township. The first return to name everyone in a household separately is 1850. Microfilm copies of the returns for Aroostook County may be viewed at the libraries of the University of Maine campuses at Fort Kent and at Presque Isle and at the Madawaska Public Library.

No table showing searchers which township to look in for another has been created to date. However, it is reasonable for searchers to look in the nearest town, with Fort Kent, Frenchville, Madawaska, and Van Buren being the most likely names to look under. From 1880 on, today's townships are all separate enumeration districts for the townships covered by this monograph.

Canadian Censuses

Canada began its federal census in 1851 and has conducted one every ten years since. The last census released is the 1901 return. Canadian censuses returns for Victoria and Madawaska Counties have been transcribed and published by Jean-Guy Poitras. Although out of print and no longer available for purchase, copies of all of them are available at the Centre de Documentation et d'Études Madawaskayenne at the University of Moncton at Edmundston and at the Acadian Archives in Fort Kent. Each return for Madawaska County is organized by civil parish.

The following table, assembled by Terrence M. Punch and George F. Sanborn* tells searchers where to look for a family in a given year. The year within parentheses is the year the civil parish was formed. The space to the right of that year indicates where one can find census data for that area in a given year. Thus, in 1851, Drummond did not yet exist as a separate civil parish and returns for that year can be found with those of Andover; in 1861, returns for the Drummond area are found with those of Grand Falls; in 1881, Drummond's returns are separate.

Drummond	(1872)	Andover	Grand Falls	Grand Falls	1881	1891
Grand Falls	(1852)	Andover	1861	1871	1881	1891
Madawaska	(1833)	1851	1861	1871	1881	1891
Sainte Anne	(1877)	Saint Léonard	and	Saint Basile	1881	1891
Saint Basile	(1850)	1851	1861	1871	1881	1891

Saint François	(1877)	1851	1861	1871	1881	1891
Saint Hilaire	(1877)	Madawaska	Madawaska	Madawaska	1881	1891
Saint Jacques	(1877)	Madawaska	Madawaska	Madawaska	1881	1891
Saint Léonard	(1850)	1851	1861	1971	1881	1891

*Source: Terrence M. Punch, C.G. and George F. Sanborn Jr., F.A.S.G., *Genealogist's Handbook for Atlantic Canada Research* (Boston: New England Historic Genealogical Society, 1997), 11. Reprinted by permission of NEHGS. All rights reserved.

Readers should take note that, in both American and Canadian censuses, the wife's surname is that of her husband. In both American and Canadian censuses, names are often mangled by a census taker who spoke only English and did his level best to record what he heard.

Miscellaneous Censuses

Three important surveys were conducted of the Valley which are useful to genealogists.

The first special census is the 1831 Deane and Kavanagh Survey commissioned by the Maine Legislature to determine the names of land holders and the source of the deed. The two men covered the entire settlement on both sides of the river. A transcript of their full report is published with an excellent introduction by W. O. Raymond in the *Collections of the New Brunswick Historical Society*, No. 9 (Saint John, Barnes, 1914), pp. 345-484. The Centre de Documentation et d'Études Madawaskayenne has this publication. The core of the report, in tabular form, is available at Chip Gagnon's web site, www.upperstjohn.com. The census is valuable for telling us who owns a lot, how large it is, and from whom the current owner purchased the lot (or whether it was a grant).

The second special census is John MacLaughlin's "Return showing the number of Inhabitants in the Settlement of Madawaska with their Stock." Filed with the New Brunswick Legislature in December 1833, the report was created for the legislature in response to requests from valley residents for relief following an unseasonably early freeze that ruined crops. The census lists every family by name of head of household, the number of children by gender in the household, t he number of each kind of stock (horses, oxen, cows, sheep, pigs), the number of tons of hay harvested, the number of bushels of seed sown last spring (wheat, barley, oats, buckwheat, peas, and potatoes), the number of bushels harvested of each crop this fall, and the average number of bushels harvested for each crop in recent past years. The report not only lists who is in the valley, but also permits comparisons with neighbors and other family members to determine each one's number of acres under cultivation and relative success. A photocopy of the document is part of the Craig Research Collection at the Acadian Archives (document MCC-00004) at the University of Maine at Fort Kent. The entire report, in tabular form, is available at Chip Gagnon's web site, www.upperstjohn.com. It is also available on microfilm at the Provincial Archives of New Brunswick and at the Centre de Documentation et d'Études Madawaskayenne at the University of Moncton at Edmundston.

The third special census is the "Recensement fait par le Rev. Pierre Stanislas Vallée Ptre Curé de St Bruno comprenant toutes les familles de la même paroisse de St Bruno." A photocopy is at the Acadian Archives at the University of Maine at Fort Kent. For those with access to the Drouin Genealogical Institute microfilm of Saint Bruno's registers, it is found beginning at p. 488 for the immediate area around Van Buren and Keegan proper, and beginning at p. 500 for surrounding rural communities. The census is after entries for the 1870s. It would appear that the "concessions" covered are in today's Caswell Plantation, Hamlin Plantation, Cyr Plantation, maybe Connors Plantation, and Van Buren Township. The census, written in a lovely hand, has columns for Localité (current sub-community name), Nombre (family number for the count of families in the parish), Nom (name of each family member with maiden name given for wives), Age (age of each person as of the month the census was taken), M (number of years the parents have been married or number of years that the head of household has been widowed), Lieu de Naisance (the community or country where a person was born), C (whether the person has made a first communion), E (whether the individual attends school), Origine (the names of both parents of the head of household and of his wife), and Occupation (of the breadwinner, almost always "Cultivateur"). The census is valuable because it identifies parents and community of residence within the townships indicated.

Land Records

There are two repositories of land deeds in the Upper Saint John River Valley, one on each side of the River.

American Side

Northern Registry of Deeds

P. O. Box 47 22 Hall Street, Suite 201
Fort Kent ME 04743-0047

207-834-3925
regofdeeds@nci2.net
www.aroostook.me.us/deeds.html
Hours: 8:00 a.m. to 4:30 p.m., Monday to Friday

How to get there:

Cross the Fish River in Fort Kent heading west on US-1. Two blocks past the Fish River bridge, US-1 bears right. Do not bear to the right; instead, go straight onto Elm Street, then one block further to the intersection of Elm and Hall Streets. The Registry is on the second floor of the red brick building on the left. Parking is available on the Hall Street side building.

About the registry:

Deeds date from 1845. All records are open to the public, and there is no user fee accessing records. Searchers do their own searches and may do their own photocopying on site for a small per-page fee. To find a record, the searcher must know the name of the party selling or buying. Deeds are indexed by grantors (sellers) and grantees (buyers) in separate books from the deeds themselves. Tax maps by township showing lots in relation to others by owners' name are available and may be photocopied as well. Staff members will do lookups for one year only and only if callers know the year. There is a fee for deeds photocopying and for mailing a deed.

The Registry's web site is only in English, but all staff members at the Northern Registry of Deeds are fully bilingual. Hours are either Eastern Standard Time or Daylight Standard Time, an hour different from the Canadian side.

Canadian Side

Registry and Mapping Services

121 rue de l'Église street
P O. Box 5001
Edmundston NB E3V 3L3

506-735-2710
rpiis.comments@snb.ca
www.gnb.ca/snb
Hours: 8:15 a.m. to 5:00 p.m., Monday to Friday

How to get there:

Cross the international bridge from Madawaska. Turn right onto Saint François, left onto Canada, then right onto rue de l'Église (Church St.). The Registry is in the Carrefour Assomption, a two-story building on the left; park on the street. The Registry and Mapping Services office is on the second floor.

About the registry:

Deeds date from 1848. All records are open to the public, and there is a user fee for each half-day of access. Searchers do their own look-ups and may do their own photocopying on site for a per-page fee. To find a record, the searcher must know the name of the party selling or buying. Deeds are indexed by grantors (sellers) and grantees (buyers) in separate books from the deeds themselves. Distant researchers may access land information via the Internet. Fees for this Real Property Information Internet Service (RPIIS) are either by-the-transaction or monthly unlimited-time use. To use this service, searchers must obtain an account with Service New Brunswick by calling 506-856-3704 or by emailing rpiis.comments@snb.ca.

Traditional paper maps have been replaced by the Custom Map Service, an electronic database. Customer Service staffers at the Registry and Mapping Services office will work with searchers to locate and print a map of a parcel. Fees for printing depend on the number of parcels printed. There is also a search fee which is waived if enough parcels are printed. Service New Brunswick is also the distributor of Crown Land Grant Maps printed by the provincial Department of Natural Resources and Energy. Crown Land Grant maps can be purchased at the Registry and Mapping Services office. The maps show lot numbers and the name of the fist owner or the owner (often a descendant) as of 1848.

Service New Brunswick's web site is fully bilingual, and all staff at all offices are fully bilingual as well. Hours are Atlantic Time, an hour different from the American side.

Wills and Probate Documents

Neither in Aroostook County nor in Madawaska County are wills required to be probated or filed in Probate Court. For much of the 19th century, all parents had to give was sweat equity, and that was the farm. Thus, the parents' final deed was typically to a son or daughter in exchange for lifetime care. These deeds are often quite detailed and fulfill the functions of a last will and testament. In Canada, wills, letters of probate, or letters of administration (but only if land is involved in a will) may be filed in the Registry and Mapping Services office, and searchers will occasionally find one there. When wills are probated or are challenged in probate court, searchers can find them.

American Side

Aroostook County Probate Court

26 Court Street, Suite 103
Houlton ME 04730

207-532-1502
joanne@aroostook.me.us
www.aroostook.me.us/probate.html
Hours: 8:00 a.m. to 4:30 p.m., Monday to Friday

How to get there:

From I-95, exit at US-1A. Drive south on US-1A to Military Street, turn east and go to the stop light at Court Street. The courthouse is at the intersection of Military and Court streets, and there is ample street parking.

About the probate court:

Probate documents are on the ground floor of the county courthouse. Records are open to the public and photocopying may be done by searchers in the registry for a nominal fee. Records are indexed in separate volumes. Documents are available from 1840-on.

Canadian Side

Probate Court of New Brunswick

Court Services–Edmundston–Grand Falls Regional Office
121 rue de l'Église Street, Room 231
P. O. Box 5001
Edmundston NB E3V 3L3

506-737-4419
www.gnb.ca/justice/index.htm

How to get there:

Cross the international bridge from Madawaska. Turn right onto Saint François, left on Canada, and right onto rue de l'Église (Church St.). The Probate Court is on the second floor of Carefour Assomption, a two story building at the corner of Victoria and Église streets. Park on the street.

About the probate court:

Wills need not be filed unless contested, submitted for validation, or involve an estate large enough to justify the appointment of an administrator. Wills filed with the court are held in Edmundston only for one or two years. Then they are sent the Provincial Archives of New Brunswick in Fredericton; when there are enough on file, they are microfilmed. PANB microfilms cover the years 1894 through 1930 and are available through inter-library loan. Post-1931 files are available only at the PANB. (PANB contact information is given below in the Archives section.) The following are the PANB and LDS numbers for those records that are on microfilm.

Period	PANB	LDS
1894-1917	F10780	1420164
1918-1924	F10781	1420165
1924-1930	F10782	1402465

Newspapers

Newspapers are a source of vital statistics through birth announcements, engagement announcements, and obituaries. However, genealogists who are trying to write family histories should also look to the news of the area in which their ancestors lived. Often, stories will mention the names of distant relatives or describe events that impacted them directly.

1. *Le Moniteur Acadien.* One of the oldest newspapers to carry news of the Upper Saint John Valley is *Le Moniteur Acadien* published with a few interruptions from 1867 to 1926 in Shediac, New Brunswick. Fortunately, Gérard Desjardins has extracted all stories pertaining to Madawaska County and has reprinted them. In *Le Madawaska Raconté par le Moniteur Acadien, 1867-1926* (Dieppe, New Brunswick, 1999), Desjardins has retyped every article dealing with the area from Grand Falls all the way up to the Saint Francis River. The 600 pages are filled with religious, economic, and political news as well as interesting stories of drownings, church burnings, and the usual marriage and death notices of prominent citizens. The text is in French. A copy of Desjardins' book is at the Acadian Archives and at the Centre de Documentation et d'Études Madawaskayenne. Copies also are available for purchase from Gérard Desjardins, 281 avenue Beaubassin, Dieppe NB E1A 1B3, or contact him at 506-389-3328 or gerardd@nbnet.nb.ca.

2. *Le Journal du Madawaska.* This newspaper was the first one published in the Upper Saint John Valley. Published in Van Buren, it ran from December 1902 through December 1906. Paper issues of the paper were bound in two volumes but have disappeared. Fortunately, a microfilm copy was made. The microfilm, titled *Le Journal du Madawaska, 1903-1905,* has all issues of the paper, and is at the Acadian Archives at the University of Maine at Fort Kent as well as at the Madawaska Public Library. The text is predominantly in French, although there are up to two pages of English-language articles. The paper contained news, serial novels, letters, humor, and advertisements.

2. *Saint John Valley Times.* This newspaper began publishing in 1957 and is on-going. It is published in Madawaska weekly on Wednesdays, almost entirely in English, although a few items have appeared in French since about 1986. It includes obituaries, and engagement or wedding announcements when the paper is apprised of them. Recent issues are available at most Valley libraries on the American side, and all back issues are available on microfilm at the Acadian Archives at the University of Maine at Fort Kent and at the Madawaska Public Library. It is not available on the web.

3. *Le Madawaska.* This newspaper began publishing in 1913 and is on-going. It is published in Edmundston weekly on Wednesdays, exclusively in French. It includes obituaries but no engagement or wedding announcements. Recent issues are available at most Valley libraries on the Canadian side, and a microfilm copy of all past issues is available at the University of Moncton Edmundston Campus library and at the Monseigneur W. J. Conway Public Library in Edmundston. The Acadian Archives at the University of Maine at Fort Kent has a microfilm copy of all issues from 1913 through

1999. The front page for the past week is available on the web at www.lemadawaska.com/madawaska/index.cfm, and visitors may view the past three weeks of death notices at the site.

4. *The Bangor Daily News–Northern Edition*. This newspaper began publishing in 1889 and is on-going. A Northern Edition has been published for the Aroostook County area, including news from the Saint John Valley, since the paper's beginning. It is a daily with Saturday and Sunday combined into one issue. Death notices are in every issue. In recent years, obituaries, engagements, and weddings have been included only at the request of families who pay by the line. It is printed exclusively in English. Recent issues are available at most Valley libraries plus the University of Maine at Fort Kent and at Presque Isle on the American side. A microfilm copy of all past issues (including regional editions) is available at the Bangor Public Library, the Maine State Library in Augusta, and the Fogler Library at the University of Maine in Orono. The paper can be accessed back to 1993 through its web site at www.bangornews.com. Obituaries are searchable for several years at the web site, and there is a fee for accessing older issues.

Archives

Acadian Archives/Archives Acadiens

23 University Drive
University of Maine at Fort Kent
Fort Kent ME 04743

207-834-7535
acadian@maine.edu
www.umfk.maine.edu/infoserv/archives
Hours: 8:00 a.m. to noon, Monday to Thursday and by appointment

How to get there:

From the intersection of US-1 and ME-11 (Main and Pleasant Streets), procede south on ME-11 0.2 miles to the University of Maine campus. The entrance is on the east side of the street immediately south of the former laboratory school. The Blake Library is on the right after entering the campus, and ample parking is available on the north of the library building.

About the archives:

The Archives collects print and audio/visual materials relevant to the history, culture, and folklife of the Upper Saint John Valley. The Archives has the standard compilations of Quebec and Acadian marriages (Tanguay, Jetté, Arsenault, PRDH, and White). It also has the original 8-volume Langlois/Lang Dictionnaire Généalogique du Madawaska as well as its Voskuhl enhancement. It has a good number of local family history / genealogies and copies of the New Brunswick Crown Land Grant maps showing lot owners for the Canadian side. It has over twenty travelers accounts of the Madawaska Settlement which provides insights into the area as seen though different pairs of eyes between 1780 and 1870. It also has the only copy of Beatrice Craig's Reconstruction Sheets of early Valley families to about 1850. Each family sheet has the names of all children, their birth dates, and their spouses. The Archives also has Béatrice Craig's Property Transfer Reconstructions from 1785 through 1850, including deeds of maintenance (lifetime care mortgages), and probated wills from 1840 through 1900. The Archives is one of two locations in the Valley where visitors can find a microfilm copy of all US census returns for Aroostook County in Maine and of all Canadian census returns for Madawaska and Victoria Counties in New Brunswick. (The University of Maine at Presque Isle is the other.) A web search engine enables individuals to search Archival material in advance of a visit, and its web site is well organized and rich in content. Archive staff respond to email inquiries. Searchers are urged to call in advance of a visit.

Centre de documentation et d'Études Madawaskayenne

Université de Moncton, campus d
Edmundston 165, boulevard Hébert
Edmundston NB E3V 2S8

506-737-5179
mtheriau@CUSLM.ca
www.cuslm.ca/cedm/
Hours: 9:00 a.m. to 5:00 p.m., Monday to Friday

How to get there:

From the Transcanada, take the Boulevard Hébert for Edmundston. The entrance to the University is on the east side of he street at the second traffic light south of the exit. Ample parking is in front of the main building of this former seminary. The CDEM is in the southeast corner of the basement of the La Rose Library in the building's west wing.

About the archives:

A unit of the Rhéa Larose Library at the University de Moncton, campus d'Edmundston, (formerly known as the Centre Universaire Saint-Louis-Maillet), the CDEM collects material on all aspects of the Madawaska area, including history, economics, and genealogy. Its broad scope means that it has microfilm, audiotape, and photographs as well as books, brochures, periodicals, government publications, and student theses. Of specific interest to the genealogist are microfilm copies all Catholic church parish registers for all parishes in the Diocese of Edmundston, and print extracts of all Madawaska and Victoria County censuses since 1851. It has a number of parish, town, and family histories, most for the Canadian side. Its web site contains a complete listing of its holdings, and the director responds to email inquiries. Searchers are urged to call in advance of a visit.

Archives de la Côte-du-Sud et du Collège de Sainte-Anne

100, 4eme avenue
La Pocatière QC G0R 1Z0

418-856-2104
grchsud@globetrotter.qc.ca
www.shcds.org

About the archives:

The Archives are the result of a merger of the Société Historique de la Côte-du-Sud and of the College's own archive. This private organization is the premier historical society for the Bas Saint Laurent. Its impressive collection includes over 200,000 photographs, 3,000 maps, and 104 rolls of microfilm. Genealogists will find microfilm copies of 51 different parish registers, civil registrations for Kamouraska County from 1685 through 1887, censuses for Kamouraska County, printed parish histories for parishes between Montmagny up to Rivière-du-Loup, marriage repertoires for the entire Côte-du-Sud, a large collection of family histories, and the standard genealogical dictionaries. Due to an agreement with the Archives Nationals de Québec, it is also the repository of a number of governmental records.

Centre d'Études Acadiennes

Edifice Champlain, Room A020-C
University of Moncton
Moncton NB E1A 3E9

506-858-4085
basquem@umoncton.ca
www.umoncton.ca/etudeacadiennes/centre/cea.html
Hours: 8:30 a.m. to 4:30 p.m., Monday to Friday; 7:00 p.m. to 10:00 p.m., Thursday
(There are no evening hours during May through August.)

About the archives:

The SEA collects any and all documentation available on every conceivable aspect
of the Acadians. That includes history, genealogy, demography, ethnology, sociology,
archeology, folklore, geography, economy, language, music, art, and culture. Its holdings
are quite extensive-over 10,000 books and over 4,000 reels of microfilm—and are listed
in one of its publications, Inventaire général des sources documentaires sur les Acadiens,
which is available for sale at the SEA Its primary value to genealogists is its collection of
microfilm copies of censuses and church registers for the 1636-1755 period before the
deportation, although it has microfilmed copies of church registers from parishes in
Québec, New Brunswick, other Canadian Maritime provinces. It also has copies of
documents pertaining to Acadians in the National Archives of Canada and in the Archives
Nationale de France. For the genealogist working on family history, the SEA has a full
run of every newspaper published for parts of the Acadian community. For the genealogist tracking Acadian families, the value of the SEA is that it has what can be found in
other national, state, and provincial archives all in one place. None of the SEA's material
circulates and must be used on site. The SEA's full-time genealogist, Stephen White, is at
work on a definitive genealogy of all Acadian families. The initial two volumes, titled
Dictionnaire Genealgoique des Familles Acadiennes, covering marriages from 1636
through 1714, are also available for sale through the SEA.

Maine Archives

84 State House Station
Augusta ME 04333-0084

207-287-5795
anne.small@state.me.us
www.state.me.us/sos/arc/
Hours: 8:00 a.m. to 4:00 p.m., Monday to Friday

How to get there:

From I-95, exit onto US-202 south at Augusta; proceed east (Western Ave.) to State
Street at the traffic circle; then go south two blocks to just past the state capital building.
The building is on the west side of the street, and parking near the capital is scant.

About the archives:

The MSA is the state's repository for official documents from 1820-on. All US
census returns for every township and county in Maine since 1790, when the state was a
part of Massachusetts, and microfilm copies of all vital statistics (birth, marriage, death)

since 1893 are among the holdings. Researchers can also view microfilm copies of Land Office surveys showing lots of individuals given land grants. For those who cannot visit the archives, MSA staff maintain a list of searchers who conduct research for a fee. Some vital statistics (marriages, 1892-1967 and 1976-1996) are searchable at its website. (Note: parents' names are not provided.) The staff responds to questions regarding specific MSA holdings by email and telephone.

Provincial Archives of New Brunswick

Bonar Law–Bennet Building
23 Dineen Drive/P. O. Box 6000
University of New Brunswick
Fredericton NB F3B 5H1

506-453-2122
ProvincialArchives@gnb.ca
www.archives.gnb.ca/Archives/EN/Default.aspx
Hours: 10:00 a.m. to 5:00 p.m., Monday to Friday; 8:30 a.m. to 5:00 p.m., Saturday

How to get there:

Exit off the Transcanada at NB-101. Drive north on NB-101 (Regent Street), turn right onto Kings College Road, and turn left onto Dineen. Parking is very limited, but several places are reserved for visitors on the south side of the building. A parking permit is required for visitors but is issued at no charge by PANB staff.

About the archives:

The PANB is the province's repository for official documents from 1784-on. Its county guides (available on-site or off its web site) are excellent finding aides, listing the microfilm number for census returns, marriage records, vital statistics, land records, church records, and family and local histories. The PANB has a number of publications for sale, including census returns for a given county and year. There is a complete collection of Crown Land Grant maps for the entire province showing lot boundaries and lot owners. A limited but increasing number of marriage and death records as well as land records are searchable on line at its web site. PANB material which is on microfilm can be borrowed via interlibrary loan. Staff respond to telephone and email requests for information about holdings. The PANB's web site is fully bilingual as are its staff.

Archives Nationals de Québec

337, rue Moreault
Rimouski QC G5L 1P4

418-727-3500
anq.rimouski@mcc.gouv.qc.ca
www.anq.gouv.qc.ca
Hours: 8:30 a.m. to 12:00 p.m. and 1:00 p.m. to 4:30 p.m., Monday to Friday

How to get there:

From the information center on Saint-Germain Ouest in downtown Rimouski, go east on Saint-Germain. The Archives are in the basement of a multi-story building of provincial offices on the south side of the street. Ample parking is available on the east side of the building.

About the archives:

The archives at Rimouski are the official repository for the Bas Saint Laurent region (which includes Kamouraska, Rivière-du-Loup, Les Basques, and Témiscouata Counties, among others). Documents held at this branch of the ANQ date from the late 1600s and include original copies of civil registers (birth, marriage, death, but only up to 1900); notarial records (which include land sales & purchases); wills (whether done by a notary or done privately and validated at superior court); and many land surveys of private property boundaries. Visitors are welcome, and no fee is charged searchers. Requests from those who cannot come to the archives must b e in writing. There is a fee for photocopying and for mailing photocopies of documents. Documents held at the ANQ can be searched through the ANQ "Pistard" search engine at the ANQ web site which is entirely in French. Likewise, visitors should be able to speak some French.

Libraries

Local libraries have always worked to serve the interests of residents in their area of service. That is certainly true in the Upper Saint John Library. In addition, the low population density means that not every library can have as extensive a collection as desired, and each of the public municipal libraries listed below permits individuals from outside its service area and from across the River to borrow materials which circulate. The policy varies somewhat from library to library, and visitors from outside a given library's service area should ask for that library's policy.

American Side

Abel J. Morneault Memorial Library

303 Maine Street
Van Buren ME 04785

207-868-5076
ajmml@morneault.lib.me.us
www.vanburenmaine.com/government/index.html
Hours: 9:00 a.m. to noon and 1:00 p.m. to 5:00 p.m., Tuesday, Thursday and Friday; 9:00 a.m. to noon and 1:00 p.m. to 8:00 p.m., Wednesday; 9:00 a.m. to 1:00 p.m., Saturday

How to get there:

The library is on south side of US-1 (Main Street) 0.2 miles west of Violet Brook and immediately to the east of the high school.

About the library:

This is Van Buren's public library. The Library's Martine A. Pelletier Special Collections Room, named for the woman who led the drive to create a public library, has a variety of useful tools for the genealogist. There are a number of family histories, most unpublished, a complete copy of Fr. Langlois Dictionnaire Généalogique du Madawaska, and several published works. The centennial history of Saint Bruno parish and of the Town of Van Buren are there as well. The most important resource, existing only here and nowhere else in its entirety, is the Martine Pelletier extract of Saint Bruno's register. Each register entry is on a separate file card. Cards are filed alphabetically by the surname of the person. Marriage entries are the exception, being filed under the groom's name only. Baptisms, marriages, and burials are in separate drawers. The extracts go from the beginning of the parish's register in 1838 through the late 1960s. The library has one of two public copies of Town Clerk Victorie Dufour's listing of births. (The other copy is at the Acadian Archives at the University of Maine at Fort Kent.) The list is made from Saint Bruno(s registers and goes from their beginning in1838 to 1893 when mandatory civil birth registrations began. Since Saint Bruno once covered both sides of the river for approximately a third of the Valley in its earliest years, both the Martine Pelletier cards and Victorie Dufour list are very important genealogical tools. Neither has been published.

Allagash Public Library

R.F.D.–Box 146
Allagash ME 04774-9701

207-398-4454
allagashlibrary@sjv.net
www.aroostook.me.us/allagash/library.html
Hours: 1:00 p.m. to close (time varies), Tuesday and Thursday; 1:00 p.m. to close (times vary), Saturday

How to get there:

The library is the second building northeast of the bridge over the Allagash River on ME-161.

About the library:

Located in part of a former grade school on the northwest side of ME-161 in Allagash, this new library, staffed by a single volunteer, has only been operational since 1999. It has no genealogy section. Closing times vary, and the library is often open on Sunday morning from 9:00 a.m. on.

Madawaska Public Library

393 Maine Street
Madawaska ME 04756

207-728-3606
madlib@nci1.net
Hours: 10:00 a.m. to 8:00 p.m., Monday to Friday; 10:00 a.m. to 3:00 p.m., Saturday

How to get there:

The library is on the south side of US-1 (Main Street) 0.3 miles east of Bridge Street.

About the library:

The Library has a separate room to support genealogical research. It contains a complete collection of the family genealogies (29 as of 2001) assembled for each of the surname family reunions held in Madawaska on the weekend of the fourth of July each summer. Each book has interesting historical vignettes of past family members, photos of recent family members, and a sizeable amount of information on the family genealogy. In addition, it has almost all family genealogies produced of valley families. The Library has several histories of Acadia and of Québec. It also has a number of standard genealogical dictionaries, an original copy of the Langlois / Lang Dictionnaire Généalogique du Madawaska, and the CD version of the Voskuhl enhancement loaded on the hard drive of a dedicated PC. The Library is the only non-university library to have microfilm copies of US census returns for Aroostook County, although they only include

1840 through 1900, and it is the only public library on the American side which has microfilm copies of many of the church registers of Catholic churches on the Canadian side of the Valley. Only at the Madawaska Public Library can searchers find all of the Léon Guimond extracts of church registers for American side Catholic churches. Most of these extracts, primarily marriage entries, have not been published, and those that have been printed have had a very limited distribution. In addition, it has the printed marriage repertoires of 15 Québec parishes. Three crammed ring binders hold donated funeral cards of individuals who died in the valley. An ignored gem is Cécile Pozzoto's large collection of valley photographs, mostly of individuals. The library wisely has several works on how to do genealogy. Two personal computers, one dedicated for Internet access, and a microfilm reader with printer support visitors.

Fort Kent Public Library

1 Monument Square
Fort Kent ME 04734

207-834-3048
mpooler@fort-kent.lib.me.us

Hours: 8:00 a.m. to 5:00 p.m., Monday, Tuesday and Thursday; 8:00 a.m. to 8:00 p.m., Wednesday and Friday

How to get there:

The library is at the intersection of ME-11 with US-1 just to the west of the stop light at the west end of the bridge over the Fish River.

About the library:

The library has 19 of the family history-genealogies assembled for surname family reunions held at Mada3waska each summer. It also has a complete copy of the original *Langlois/Lang Dictionnaire Généalogique du Madawaska,* and the centennial publications for Fort Kent, Madawaska, and Van Buren.

University of Maine at Presque Isle Library

181 Main Street
Presque Isle ME 04769-2888

207-768-9599
roe@umpi.maine.edu
www.umpi.maine.edu

Hours: 8:00 a.m. to 10:00 p.m., Monday to Thursday; 8:00 a.m. to 4:30 p.m., Friday; noon to 4:30 p.m., Saturday; 2:00 p.m. to 9:00 p.m., Sunday

How to get there:

The campus is on the west side of US-1 on the south lip of the Aroostook River Valley. The library is to the west of the president's house and is accessed by the circle drive around campus. Parking is on the southwest side of the library building. Hours given above are those for the fall and spring semesters when classes are in session.

About the library:

The Special Collections area of the UMPI Library maintains a number of items useful to the genealogist. Although there is no good, comprehensive history of Aroostook County, the Library has almost all books published about the county, has individual town histories, and maintains vertical files with clippings on the County from newspapers. The Library also maintains a collection of family histories, including some never published, on County families. The Special Collections area is one of three in the County that a researcher can go to find a microfilm copy of all US census returns for Aroostook County. (The Acadian Archives at the University of Maine at Fort Kent and the Madawaska Public Library are the other two.)

Canadian Side

Hours given for the following four libraries are their winter hours. All four are open for additional hours in the summer months. Patrons may access hours of operation, along with other information, through the New Brunswick Public Library Service website at http://vision.gnb.ca. (Click on Library Information, then on the map of the Upper Saint John Region, then on the name of a given library.) The web site also has a searchable catalog of holdings which identifies which libraries have a given title.

Mgr. Plourde Public Library

15 Bellevue Street
Saint François NB E7A 1A4

506-992-6052
stfplib@gnb.nb.ca
www.gnb.ca/0003/stfrancois.html
Hours: 10:00 a.m. to 12:00 p.m., 1:00 p.m. to 5:00 p.m., 6:30 p.m. to 8:30 p.m., Tuesday; 10:00 a.m. to 12:00 p.m., 1:00 p.m. to 5:00 p.m., Wednesday and Friday; 1:00 p.m. to 5:00 p.m., 6:30p to 4:30p.m., Thursday

How to get there:

From the church of Saint François-Xavier on NB-205, go west 0.1 mile, turn left onto rue Bellevue. The library is 0.1 mile ahead and on the right.

About the library:

The Mgr. Plourde Public Library has little in the area of genealogy. It has the Stephen White dictionary of acadian families plus the Charette and Kennedy family genealogies.

Mgr. W.-J.-Conway Public Library

33 Irène Street
Edmundston NB E3V 1B7

506-735-4713
biblioed@gnb.ca
www.gnb.ca/0003/edmundston.html
Hours: noon to 8:30 p.m., Tuesday and Thursday; 10:30 a.m. to 5:00 p.m., Wednesday; 9:00 a.m. to 5:00 p.m.,Friday and Saturday

About the library:

Visitors must surrender a photo identificaton, such as a driver's license in order to access the Heritage Room. There, searchers will find microfilm copies of almost every parish register in the Upper Saint John Valley on the Canadian side. Microfilm copies of Canadian censuses for Madawaska County are available from 1851 though 1891 along with Poitras' published extracts through 1901. Standard genealogical dictionaries (Tanguay, Jetté), genealogies (White, Arsenault), and marriage repertoires (Proulx, Langlois/Lang, Poitras) are in the room. About a dozen family genealogies are in the collection, likely of families that have lived in the Saint-Jacques, Edmundston, Saint-Basile area. Several area parish and community centennial histories round them out. A full run of Le Madawaska through 1992 is available on microfilm, and a copy of Desjardins' book providing all articles dealing with the Upper Saint John Valley and published in le Moniteur Acadien is in the room. Librarians have wisely acquired several works on doing genealogy.

Dr. Lorne J. Violette Public Library

180 St-Jean Street
Saint Léonard NB E7E 2B9

506-423-3025
stlplib@gnb.ca
www.gnb.ca/0003/stleonard.html
Hours: 10:00 a.m. to 5:00 p.m., 6:30 p.m. to 8:30 p.m., Tuesday and Thursday; 10:00 a.m. to 5:00 p.m., Wednesday and Friday; 11:00 a.m. to 4:00 p.m., Saturday

About the library:

The library's genealogy materials are mostly the gift of Sr. Marguerite Cyr who, for many years, operated a modest Centre de Recherches Généalogique at the Marist Convent at Saint-Léonard-Parent. All genealogical materials are housed in a side room. They include the standard genealogical dictionaries of Québec, White's dictionary of Acadian families, the Poitras repertoire of valley marriages, and the Proulx repertoire of Kamouraska County marriages. The collection includes several area parish and community centennial histories. Visitors will also find the printed genealogies of several families from the Van Buren and Saint Léonard area. Several personal computers, including one dedicated to Internet use, support visitors.

Grand Falls Public Library

131 Pleasant Street, Suite 201
Grand Falls NB E3Z 1G6

506-475-7781
gfplib@gnb.ca
www.gnb.ca/0003/grandfalls.html
Hours: noon to 8:00 p.m., Tuesday and Thursday; 9:00 a.m. to 5:00 p.m., Wednesday and Friday; 11:00 a.m. to 4:00 p.m., Saturday

About the library:

Visitors will need to ask a staff member at the circulation desk to unlock the handsome book case that holds the genealogy materials, many of them typescript. The collection contains several books on how to do genealogy, along with printed copies of the finding aids for every county in New Brunswick prepared by the Provincial Archives of New Brunswick. Visitors will find all of the Canadian census extracts for Madawaska and Victoria counties published by Poitras as well as many official census reports for Glouchester, Carleton, Restigouche, and Victoria counties. About a dozen family genealogies are included as are the standard genealogical dictionaries (Tanguay, Jetté, White, Arsenault) and a good collection of marriage repertoires, including the Langlois/ Lang and Poitras publications for the Upper Saint John Valley, but also a typed version of Martine Pelletier's extracts of Saint Bruno marriages, Carboneau's repertoire for the entire diocese of Rimouski, and those for Kamouraska, Islet, and Montmagny counties on the Bas Saint Laurent. The strength of the collection comes from donations of the Grand Falls Genealogy Club, which has made typed lists of headstones in area cemeteries (Drummond through Saint Léonard), assembled a large collection of donated funeral cards, and a typed extract of baptisms and Assomption parish. The library's list of holdings of interest to genealogists is available through the "Genealogy Reference" link at www.rootsweb.com/~nbgfgc/, the Grand Falls Genealogy Club web site.

Museums

Museums have as their core function preserving evidence of our past and interpreting it for future generations. The following all have clues as to how our ancestors lived. All are staffed by volunteers, and hours of operation may vary from summer to summer. (All are closed during the winter months.) To find out when a given museum is open, visitors should visit the nearest public library or town office.

Acadian Village

US-1 Keegan ME 04785

Allagash Museum

Saint John River Bridge
Allagash, ME 04774

Boutique de la Forge Joseph B. Michaud

7, rue Bellevue
Saint-François-de-Madawaska, NB E7A 1A4

Grand Falls Museum

P. O. Box 1572
Grand Falls NB E0J 1M0

Historical Caboose & Water Tower

US-1
Frenchville ME 04745

Musée Culturel du Mont-Carmel

US-1
Lille ME 04749

Musée de Madawaska

165 Blvd. Hébert
Edmundston NB E3V 2S8

Sainte Agathe Historical House

534 Main Street
Saint Agatha ME 04772

Tante Blanche Museum

US-1
Madawaska ME 04756

Pioneer Historical Museum

3614 NB-205
Connors NB E7A 1S3

Historical Societies

Genealogy is often a matter of connecting with others of like interests. When searchers find the geographic area their ancestors lived in, it is often helpful to contact individuals who live in that area. Often they will have a wealth of information on local families that they will share gladly.

Allagash Historical Society
RFD-1, Box 237
Allagash ME 04774

Madawaska Historical Society
393 Main St.
Madawaska ME 04756

Société Historique du Madawaska
P. O. Box 474
Edmundston NB E3V 3L1

Grand Falls Historical Society
P. O. Box 1572
Grand Falls NB E0J 1M0

Pioneers Historical Society of Connors
Connors NB E0L 1J0

Société Historique de Clair
326, rue Principal
Claire NB E0L 1B0

Fort Kent Historical Society
ME-161 at US-1
Fort Kent, ME 04743

La Société Historique de la Côté-du-Sud
100, 4e avenue Painchaud
La Pocatière G0R 1Z0

Genealogy Clubs

Clubs are associations of like-minded people doing the same kind of thing. The following two clubs have produced materials which can save searchers hours of work and help them significantly advance their research. Searchers working to assemble the genealogy of a family that lived in the Upper Saint John Valley should connect with each of these to locate individuals who are working on one or another line of their families.

Grand Falls Genealogy Club

c/o Anne Côté
142, rue Court
Grand-Sault NB E3Z 2R2

506-473-4881
annec@nb.sympatico.ca
www.rootsweb.com/~nbgfgc/

The club meets in the Grand Falls Public Library, in the Municipal Complex, at 131 Pleasant Street, diagonally across the street from Assomption church, every second Tuesday of the month at 6:00 p.m. The annual membership fee is modest. An email list keeps members informed of club activities. The club has created search aids that visitors can benefit from, including typing lists of cemetery headstones for all cemeteries in the Grand Falls and Saint Léonard area (which are also available through the "Cemetery Transcriptions" link on the club's web site), typed up extracts of the registers of Saint Basile (marriages), Saint Bruno (marriages), and Assomption (births, marriages, burials). The club has also acquired several family genealogies and local parish and community histories. These materials are available for visitors to use in the back room of the Grand Falls Museum whenever the museum is open. Other items the club has created are housed at the Grand Falls Public Library and are described in the Libraries section. One is a list of members with contact information and the families they research.

Société de Généalogique et d'Archives de Rimouski

110, rue de l'Évêché Est
Rimouski QC G5L 1X9

418-724-3242
sgarimouski@quebectel.com
www.genealogie.org/club/sgar

The Society's holdings are housed in a basement room of the Bibliothèque Lisette-Morin located at the corner of Belzille and l'Évêché Est in Rimouski. The room is accessed by a side entrance to the basement. Formerly called the Société généalogique de l'est du Québec, it is the largest genealogical society outside of Québec City. The SGAR is an excellent example of what a fee-for-membership organization can do. Its collection of published parish repertoires includes not only marriages but many baptisms (births) and burials(deaths) as well. The collection includes all Bas Saint-Laurent parishes and many of those published for Francophone parishes in New Brunswick (including the Upper Saint John Valley's Langlois/Lang index and Poitras' listing), Maine, New Hampshire, and a few other locales. The collection's wide scope permits searchers to trace Québec families who moved to New England farms and cities. The SGAR's collection of genealogical dictionaries includes all the standards, but its gem is a complete set of the Drouin Genealogy Institute books (49 for men, 64 for women). Its collection of community and parish histories includes at least one from the Upper Saint John Valley (Immaculate Conception). Four microfilm readers-one connected to a printer-three personal computers for software searches, and a photocopier (use is free) support visitors. The published repertoires are well indexed, and an index is under development for parish and town histories. The microfilm collection includes all of the Drouin documents, all civil registrations in Québec through 1940, and many of he microfilms made by the LDS of church registers. Software loaded on SGAR's personal computers include search engines for exploring a number of databases. They include the composite database of all repertoires printed by all genealogy societies in the Province of Québec, a database of all notarial acts from 1633 to present, the complete database from the Programme de Reserche en Démographie Historique (PRDH), and a data bank of civil marriages and deaths from 1926 through 1996. Members may use the library for free; non-members pay a modest per-day fee. Searchers working on the Québec side of their families will find the expense for several nights at an area bed and breakfast well worth it in order to spend a few days at this excellent resource.

Related Resource Publications

Many Upper Saint John Valley residents moved away to the mill towns of the New England states. In addition, many families with roots in the Valley also have roots outside the Valley in other Atlantic Canadian provinces. Finally, almost all the Acadian families with roots in the Valley have intermarried Canadian families with roots in Québec. Thus, the following resources are worth using by searchers wanting information on their families both before they arrived in the Valley and after they left it. The books tell searchers where to go for information about their family and give them an overview of what they will find when they get there. They are standards that are updated periodically and are generally available. The Punch and Sanborn, and the Melnyk are available only at the University of Maine at Fort Kent; no other library or archive in the Upper Saint John Valley has a copy of these titles. However, they are widely available at larger public and university libraries elsewhere.

> Punch, Terrence M. and George F. Sanborn. *Genealogist's Handbook for Atlantic Canada Research.* 2nd ed. Boston: New England Historic Genealogical Society, 1997.

Excellent chapters describe genealogical resources in New Brunswick and Nova Scotia, where all Acadians from the Upper Saint John Valley have roots. (Depending on the family, many Acadians who can trace themselves to the Upper Saint John Valley have roots in the other Maritime Provinces as well.) Chapter subheadings include major repositories, vital records, census records, land records, probate records, church records, immigration, newspapers, and societies and libraries. A bibliography follows each chapter. The little book is especially valuable because it contains a chapter written by Stephen A. White on Acadians. White is the genealogist at the Centre d'Études Acadiennes at the University of Moncton in New Brunswick. Acadian descendants who attempt to construct a genealogy of their ancestors must read this chapter which describes resources going back as early as 1671 and tells searchers where to find print and microfilm copies of them.

> Melnyk, Marcia D. *Genealogist's Handbook for New England Research.* 4th ed. Boston, Mass.: New England Historic Genealogical Society, 1999.

The NEHGS has improved and updated this book since it was first published twenty years ago. It lists counties (when each county was founded and what other county each was separated from) and towns (when founded and from when vital records date). A map of townships is essential for anyone trying to read census data. There are sections on vital records, federal and state censuses, probate and land records by county, cemetery records, church records, military records, immigration and naturalization, newspapers, civil and criminal court records, libraries, LDS (Mormon) Family History Centers, societies, periodicals, and books. The primary value of the book is to tell searchers where to go look for things.

Baxter, Angus. *In Search of Your Canadian Roots: Tracing Your Family Tree in Canada*. 3rd ed. rev. Baltimore,Md.: Genealogical Publishing Company, 2000.

This classic is basic for doing research on Canadian families. The book's most useful chapters are the three on Acadians, New Brunswick, and Québec. Baxter's focus is on informing readers of the locations of major research repositories followed by some of the information held at each. Major headings for the New Brunswick chapter are civil registration, provincial archives, census returns, wills, land records, genealogical societies, church registers, libraries, LDS church, and historical societies. Major headings for the Québec chapter are civil registration, the National Archives of Québec (which lists the nine regional centers), the period of New France, the period of Lower Canada and Québec, censuses, notarial deeds, wills, land records, genealogical societies, church registers, directories and newspapers, and the Montréal Central Library. As with Melnyk's book, the Baxter book's primary value is telling searchers where to go to find information and an overview of what they will find when they get there.

Selected Web Sites

There are a host of web resources supporting genealogical research on Acadian and French-Canadian families. Five of them are listed here. Two focus on the Upper Saint John Valley. Two others listed here have resource material of direct relevance to genealogists researching families that lived in the Valley. A fifth one lists the baptismal, marriage, and burial entries from one of the valley's parishes, and a final one leads to the histories of parishes that are now part of the diocese of Edmundston. As is almost always the case, these sites lead to many others. A full list of web sites supporting research on Acadians and French Canadians can be found at Cyndi's List, www.cyndislist.com/acadian.htm.

Madawaska County Genealogy

www.rootsweb.com/~mearoost/madawaska/

This web site, part of the Canada GenWeb project, provides the usual history and geography with lists of towns, rivers, etc. It provides links to GenWeb sites for adjacent New Brunswick counties with links to the main GenWeb sites of New Brunswick, Quebec, and Maine. Through them, one can reach the rootsweb sites for Restigouche County and for the lower Saint Lawrence (le Bas Saint Laurent). One page lists each church in Madawaska County with the years covered by the PANB microfilm copy of its register. Other links go to the web sites of the National Archives of Canada (NAC) and the Provincial Archives of New Brunswick. At the PANB website, one can search the marriage Register Index on line. (Not all years are available.) There also is information on where to go for census records and land records. Finally, a set of links take visitors to a number of area family web sites as well as to several of the more popular web sites supporting Acadian, French-Canadian, and Franco-American genealogy.

Aroostook County Genealogy

www.rootsweb.com/~mearoost/

This web site, part of the US GenWeb project, is well organized with tabs along the top of the opening screen to enable visitors to move around the site. A helpful site map enables visitors to locate what they seek quickly. The census page has links to transcriptions of the 1850 (partial) and of the 1860 (complete) US censuses of Aroostook County. The genealogies, family histories, and diaries page has 17 links to specific families, 13 links devoted geographical areas (mostly specific towns), and six links devoted to ways of life. The resources page lists organizations, published marriage compilations, newspapers, newsgroups, mailing lists, and 13 sites devoted to Aroostook County.

Acadian Archives

www.umfk.maine.edu/infoserv/archives/welcome.htm

Although described in a previous section of this book, the Acadian Archives has a page on Selected Links organized under the headings of Acadian History & Genealogy,

Regional History and Genealogy, Selected Archives and Libraries, French Sites in North America, Geographic Name Searches, and Regional Worldwide Web Indexes. Genealogists working on valley families will find it worth the time to visit this site.

The Upper Saint John River Valley

www.upperstjohn.com

Of all web sites devoted to supporting Acadian and French-Canadian genealogical research, this may be one having the largest quantity of original data supporting research on Upper Saint John Valley families all in one place. Major sections include censuses (1820 through 1860 transcribed by township, each with an index), land grants (1787, 1790, and 1794 plus the 1831 Deane/Kavanagh survey and the 1833 MacLaughlin survey), maps, thumbnail histories of every town or township in the region, histories of the region, and miscellaneous other records (including the names of all pastors who served Saint Basile from 1786 through 1857). For each page, there is a full footnote citing the source. In a time when anyone can put anything on the web, Chip Gagnon, this site's creator, deserves a blue ribbon for his dedication to presenting the raw data that searchers can only find in archives or on microfilm.

Assomption Parish

www.geocities.com/heartland/8787/histor.htm

This is the only parish on either side of the river which has attempted to load its registers onto the Internet. Baptisms are available from 1869 through 1920, marriages from 1869 through 1895, and burials from 1868 through 1920. In addition, there are pages listing all pastors who have served the parish from the time it was a chapel (1854), an extract of information from extant stones in the older cemetery, and an early history of the parish. Individuals with ancestors who lived within Assomption's boundaries will want to go to this site

Afterword

Every effort has been made to be inclusive and accurate. If you find an error or significant omission, please write or email the author so that a correction can be made for the next printing.

George L. Findlen
1008 Rutledge Court
Madison WI 53703-3824

findleng@tds.net